WORKING PAPERS FOR EXERCISES, PROBLEMS, AND SELECTED CASES

VOLUME 1:   CHAPTERS 1–18 AND APPENDIXES A–C

PRINCIPLES OF ACCOUNTING

2002e

Belverd E. Needles, Jr.
DePaul University

Marian Powers
Northwestern University

Susan V. Crosson
Santa Fe Community College, Florida

HOUGHTON MIFFLIN COMPANY   BOSTON   NEW YORK

Senior Sponsoring Editor: Bonnie Binkert
Senior Development Editor: Margaret M. Kearney
Associate Project Editor: Claudine Bellanton
Senior Manufacturing Coordinator: Priscilla J. Bailey
Marketing Manager: Steven Mikels

Printed in the U.S.A.

ISBN: 0-618-12428-4

3456789-POO-05 04 03 02

NOTE TO STUDENTS

This book contains Working Papers to be used in preparing solutions to all Exercises, Problems, and selected cases in Chapters 1–18 of *Principles of Accounting,* 2002e. The Working Papers are designed to simplify your work; appropriate forms for computational assignments for each exercise and problem are provided, and some preliminary information has been printed to help you get started. Items requiring extensive written responses should be word processed or submitted on lined paper.

We have occasionally provided hints on the placement of data. This is usually done only once on a page. You can infer from these hints where to enter subsequent data on that page so that it can be displayed and calculated correctly.

Accounting Format Guide

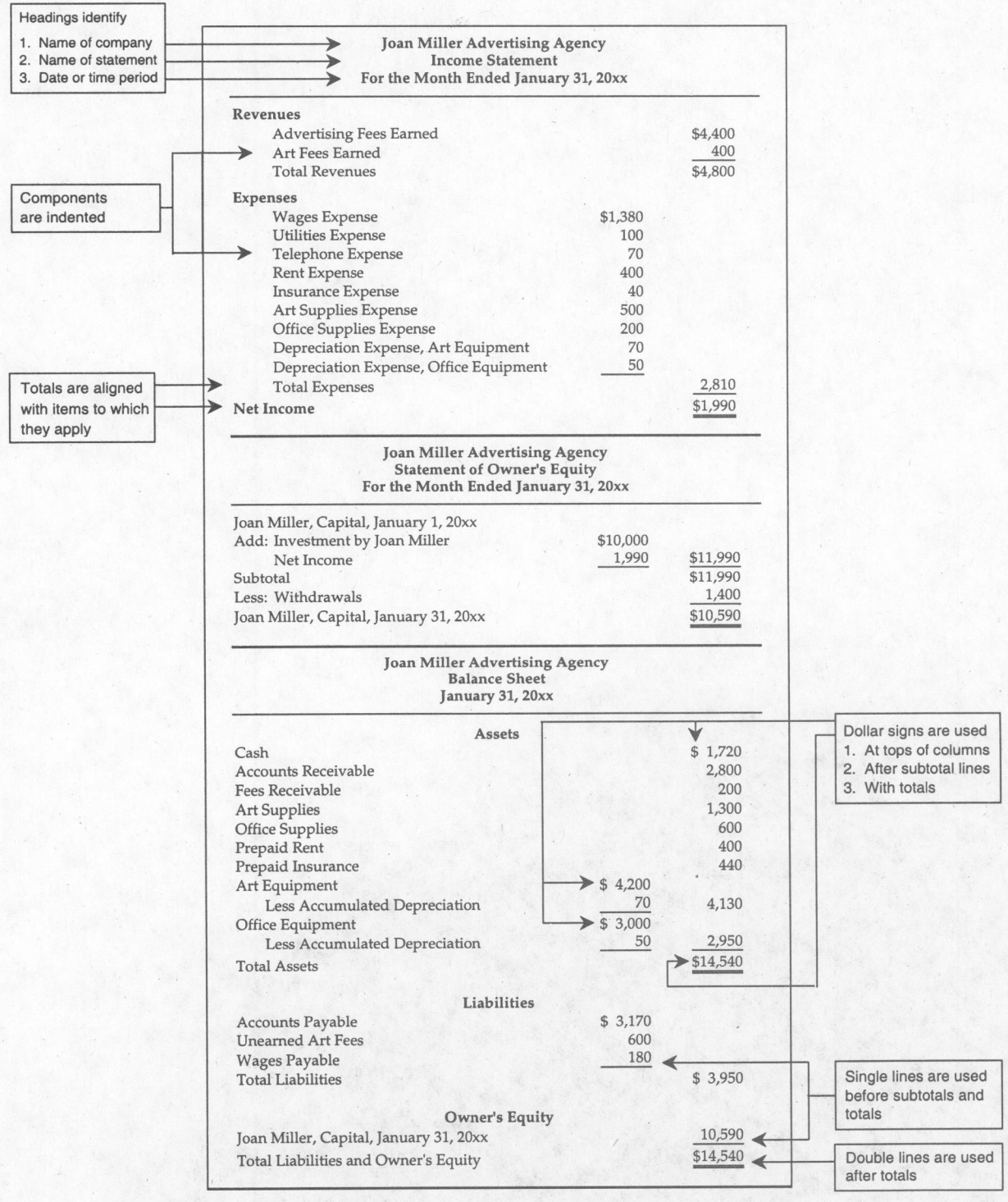

Headings identify
1. Name of company
2. Name of statement
3. Date or time period

Joan Miller Advertising Agency
Income Statement
For the Month Ended January 31, 20xx

Revenues		
Advertising Fees Earned		$4,400
Art Fees Earned		400
Total Revenues		$4,800

Components are indented

Expenses		
Wages Expense	$1,380	
Utilities Expense	100	
Telephone Expense	70	
Rent Expense	400	
Insurance Expense	40	
Art Supplies Expense	500	
Office Supplies Expense	200	
Depreciation Expense, Art Equipment	70	
Depreciation Expense, Office Equipment	50	
Total Expenses		2,810
Net Income		$1,990

Totals are aligned with items to which they apply

Joan Miller Advertising Agency
Statement of Owner's Equity
For the Month Ended January 31, 20xx

Joan Miller, Capital, January 1, 20xx		
Add: Investment by Joan Miller	$10,000	
Net Income	1,990	$11,990
Subtotal		$11,990
Less: Withdrawals		1,400
Joan Miller, Capital, January 31, 20xx		$10,590

Joan Miller Advertising Agency
Balance Sheet
January 31, 20xx

Assets		
Cash		$ 1,720
Accounts Receivable		2,800
Fees Receivable		200
Art Supplies		1,300
Office Supplies		600
Prepaid Rent		400
Prepaid Insurance		440
Art Equipment	$ 4,200	
Less Accumulated Depreciation	70	4,130
Office Equipment	$ 3,000	
Less Accumulated Depreciation	50	2,950
Total Assets		$14,540

Dollar signs are used
1. At tops of columns
2. After subtotal lines
3. With totals

Liabilities		
Accounts Payable	$ 3,170	
Unearned Art Fees	600	
Wages Payable	180	
Total Liabilities		$ 3,950

Single lines are used before subtotals and totals

Owner's Equity		
Joan Miller, Capital, January 31, 20xx		10,590
Total Liabilities and Owner's Equity		$14,540

Double lines are used after totals

Chapter 1, SE 1.

1.		4.	
2.		5.	
3.			

Chapter 1, SE 2.

1.	Assets	=	
2.	Owner's Equity	=	
3.	Liabilities	=	

Chapter 1, SE 3.

1.		=		+		
		=		+		
		−		=		
	Owner's Equity	=				
2.		=	0.2	Assets	+	
		=				
		=				
	Assets	=		+		
	Assets	=				
	Liabilities	=		×		=

Chapter 1, SE 4.

1.	Beginning:		=		+
			=		
			=		+
	Change:				
			=		+
	End:	Owner's Equity	=		
2.	Beginning:		=		+
			=		
			=		+
	Change:				
			=		+
	End:	Owner's Equity	=		

Chapter 1, SE 5.

1.	Net income	=					
		−		=			
2.	Net income	=					
	(	−		)	−		=
3.	Net income	=					
	(	−		)	+		=

Chapter 1, SE 6.

Net income	=							
(	−		)	−		+		=

Chapter 1, SE 7.

	Assets	Liabilities	Owner's Equity	
1.				
2.				
3.				
4.				
5.				
6.				

Chapter 1, SE 8.

	Assets	Liabilities	Owner's Equity	
1.				
2.				
3.				
4.				
5.				
6.				

Chapter 1, SE 9.

DeLay Company Balance Sheet June 30, 20x1			
Assets		**Liabilities**	
		Owner's Equity	

Chapter 1, E 1.

1.		5.		9.	
2.		6.		10.	
3.		7.		11.	
4.		8.		12.	

Chapter 1, E 2.

1.

2.

3.

4.

Chapter 1, E 3.

1.		6.	
2.		7.	
3.		8.	
4.		9.	
5.		10.	

Chapter 1, E 4.

Company	Sales			Assets		
Inchip						
Wong	x 0.577	=		x 0.577	=	
Mitzu	x	=		x	=	
Works	x	=		x	=	

_____ is the largest in terms of sales, and _____ is the largest in terms of assets.

Chapter 1, E 5.

1.	**Assets**	=		+				
		=		+				
	Liabilities	=						
2.	**Assets**	=		+				
	Assets	=		+				
	Assets	=						
3.	**Assets**	=		+				
	2/3 Assets	=						
	Assets	=						
	Liabilities	=	1/3	x			=	
4.	**Beginning:**		=		+			
			=					
			=		+			
	Change:							
			=		+			
	End:	**Owner's Equity**	=					

Chapter 1, E 6.

a.		d.		g.	
b.		e.		h.	
c.		f.			

Chapter 1, E 7.

	Assets	Liabilities	Owner's Equity	
a.				
b.				
c.				
d.				
e.				
f.				
g.				
h.				
i.				
j.				

Chapter 1, E 8.

1.	
2.	
3.	
4.	
5.	

Chapter 1, E 9.

		Assets	=	Liabilities	+	Owner's Equity	
1.	**Net income is:**						
	End:		=		+		
	Beginning:		=		+		
	Net income						

2.	**Net income is:**		
	Change in Owner's Equity		
	+ Owner's withdrawals		
	Net income		
3.	**Net income is:**		
	Change in Owner's Equity		
	– Owner's investment		
	Net income		
4.	**Net income is:**		
	Change in Owner's Equity		
	+ Owner's withdrawals		
	– Owner's investment		
	Net income		

Chapter 1, E 10.

1.		2.	

Chapter 1, E 11.

Bell Company		
Balance Sheet		
June 30, 20xx		
Assets		**Liabilities**
		Owner's Equity

Chapter 1, E 12.

Income Statement	Set A		Set B		Set C	
Revenues	$1,100			(g)	$340	
Expenses		(a)	5,200			(m)
Net Income		(b)		(h)	$180	
Statement of Owner's Equity						
Beginning Balance	$2,900		$15,400		$200	
Net Income		(c)	1,600			(n)
Less Withdrawals	200			(i)		(o)
Ending Balance	$3,000			(j)		(p)
Balance Sheet						
Total Assets		(d)	$21,000			(q)
Liabilities	$1,600		$ 5,000			(r)
Owner's Equity		(e)		(k)	380	
Total Liabilities and Owner's Equity		(f)		(l)	$580	

Wagoner Company
Income Statement
For the Year Ended June 30, 20x2

Revenues

Expenses

Net Income

Wagoner Company
Statement of Owner's Equity
For the Year Ended June 30, 20x2

Wagoner Company
Balance Sheet
June 30, 20x2

Assets		Liabilities
		Owner's Equity

Chapter 1, E 14.

Buena Company
Statement of Cash Flows
For the Year Ended December 31, 20x2

Cash Flows from Operating Activities		
Cash Flows from Investing Activities		
Cash Flows from Financing Activities		
Net Increase (Decrease) in Cash		

Chapter 1, E 15.

AICPA:	
SEC:	
GAAP:	
FASB:	
IRS:	
GASB:	
IASC:	
IMA:	
CPA:	

1. Accounts arranged in equation form
2. Effects of transactions shown

	Assets				=	Liabilities	+	Owner's Equity	
	Cash	Accounts Receivable	Framing Supplies	Store Equipment		Accounts Payable		Brenda Kuzma, Capital	Type of OE Transaction
a.									
bal.									
b.									
bal.									
c.									
bal.									
d.									
bal.									
e.									
bal.									
f.									
bal.									
g.									
bal.									
h.									
bal.									
i.									
bal.									
j.									
bal.									

Chapter 1, P 1. (Continued)

3. **Cash flow effects discussed**

1. Accounts arranged in equation form
2. Effects of transactions shown

	Assets				=	Liabilities	+	Owner's Equity	
	Cash	Accounts Receivable	Delivery Supplies	Motorbike		Accounts Payable		Hector Moreno, Capital	Type of OE Transaction
a.									Owner's Investment
b.									
bal.									
c.									
bal.									
d.									
bal.									
e.									
bal.									
f.									
bal.									
g.									
bal.									
h.									
bal.									
i.									
bal.									

Chapter 1, P 3.

1. Accounts arranged in equation form
2. Beginning balances entered
3. Effects of transactions shown

	Assets					=	Liabilities	+	Owner's Equity	
	Cash	Accounts Receivable	Office Supplies	Office Equipment			Accounts Payable		Delia Chan, Capital	Type of OE Transaction
bal.										
a.										
bal.										
b.										
bal.										
c.										
bal.										
d.										
bal.										
e.										
bal.										
f.										
bal.										
g.										
bal.										
h.										
bal.										
i.										
bal.										
j.										
bal.										
k.										
bal.										

Lerner Plumbing Company
Income Statement
For the Month Ended June 30, 20xx

Revenues			
Expenses			
Net Income			

Lerner Plumbing Company
Statement of Owner's Equity
For the Month Ended June 30, 20xx

M. Lerner, Capital, June 1, 20xx			
Add:			
Subtotal			

Lerner Plumbing Company
Balance Sheet
June 30, 20xx

Assets		Liabilities	
		Owner's Equity	

Chapter 1, P 5.

1. Accounts arranged in equation form

2. Effects of transactions shown

	Assets				=	Liabilities	+	Owner's Equity	
	Cash	Accounts Receivable	Supplies	Copier		Accounts Payable		L. Friedman, Capital	Type of OE Transaction
a.									
b.									
bal.									
c.									
bal.									
d.									
bal.									
e.									
bal.									
f.									
bal.									
g.									
bal.									
h.									
bal.									
i.									
bal.									
j.									
bal.									
k.									
bal.									
l.									
bal.									

17

3. | Financial statements prepared

| Royal Copying Service |
| Income Statement |
| For the Month Ended July 31, 20xx |

Revenues

Expenses

Net Income

| Royal Copying Service |
| Statement of Owner's Equity |
| For the Month Ended July 31, 20xx |

Add:

| Royal Copying Service |
| Balance Sheet |
| July 31, 20xx |

| **Assets** | | | **Liabilities** |

Owner's Equity

Chapter 1, P 6.

1. **Accounts arranged in equation form**
2. **Effects of transactions shown**

	Assets					=	Liabilities	+	Owner's Equity	
	Cash	Accounts Receivable	Supplies	Equipment	Systems Library		Accounts Payable		Carmen Vega, Capital	Type of OE Transaction
a.										
b.										
bal.										
c.										
bal.										
d.										
bal.										
e.										
bal.										
f.										
bal.										
g.										
bal.										
h.										
bal.										
i.										
bal.										
j.										
bal.										

19

Chapter 1, P 6. (Continued)

3. Cash flow effects discussed

Chapter 1, P 7.

1. Accounts arranged in equation form
2. Effects of transactions shown

	Assets				=	Liabilities	+	Owner's Equity	
	Cash	Accounts Receivable	Trucks	Equipment		Accounts Payable		Henry Redmond, Capital	Type of OE Transaction
a.									
b.									
bal.									
c.									
bal.									
d.									
bal.									
e.									
bal.									
f.									
bal.									
g.									
bal.									
h.									
bal.									
i.									
bal.									

21

1. Accounts arranged in equation form
2. Effects of transactions shown

	Assets				=	Liabilities	+	Owner's Equity	
	Cash	Accounts Receivable	Uniforms	Taxi		Accounts Payable		Suzy Maguire, Capital	Type of OE Transaction
a.									
b.									
bal.									
c.									
bal.									
d.									
bal.									
e.									
bal.									
f.									
bal.									
g.									
bal.									
h.									
bal.									
i.									
bal.									
j.									
bal.									
k.									
bal.									
l.									
bal.									

3.   **Financial statements prepared**

Dependable Taxi Service		
Income Statement		
For the Month Ended April 30, 20xx		
Revenues		
Expenses		
Net Income		

Dependable Taxi Service		
Statement of Owner's Equity		
For the Month Ended April 30, 20xx		
Add:		

Dependable Taxi Service			
Balance Sheet			
April 30, 20xx			
Assets		**Liabilities**	
		Owner's Equity	

Chapter 1, SD 5.

1. Balance sheets prepared

Henderson Lawn Care Company
Balance Sheet
June 1, 20xx

Assets		Liabilities	
		Owner's Equity	

Henderson Lawn Care Company
Balance Sheet
August 31, 20xx

Assets		Liabilities	
		Owner's Equity	

2. Net income or loss explained and computed

Chapter 1, SD 5. (Continued)

3. Recordkeeping system discussed

Chapter 2, SE 1.

Jan.	10	
Feb.	15	
Mar.	1	

Chapter 2, SE 2.

a.		e.	
b.		f.	
c.		g.	
d.		h.	

Chapter 2, SE 3.

a.		e.	
b.		f.	
c.		g.	
d.		h.	

Chapter 2, SE 4.

May	2	
	5	
	7	
	19	
	22	
	25	
	31	

Chapter 2, SE 5.

Cash							Accounts Receivable						
May	2	5,000											
Bal.													

Supplies							Office Equipment						

Accounts Payable							Unearned Programming Service Revenue						

Joe Hurley, Capital							Programming Service Revenue						

Rent Expense						

Chapter 2, SE 6.

Hurley's Programming Service
Trial Balance
May 31, 20x1

Chapter 2, SE 7.

Sanders Boating Service		
Trial Balance		
January 31, 20x1		

Chapter 2, SE 8.

General Journal					Page 4
Date	Description		Post. Ref.	Debit	Credit
20xx					
Sept. 6					
16					

Chapter 2, SE 9.

Cash

Account No. 111

Date		Item	Post. Ref.	Debit	Credit	Balance Debit	Balance Credit
20xx							
Sept.	16						

Accounts Receivable

Account No. 113

Date		Item	Post. Ref.	Debit	Credit	Balance Debit	Balance Credit
Sept.	6						
	16						

Service Revenue

Account No. 411

Date		Item	Post. Ref.	Debit	Credit	Balance Debit	Balance Credit
20xx							
Sept.	6						

Chapter 2, E 1.

Feb.	17
Mar.	7
Apr.	28
May	19
June	27

Chapter 2, E 2.

1. Purchases recognized on date shipped

Order	Date Shipped	Date Received		Amount
		Total May purchases		

2. Purchases recognized on date received

Order	Date Shipped	Date Received		Amount
		Total May purchases		

Chapter 2, E 3.

Item	Type of Account							Normal Balance (increases balance)	
			Owner's Equity						
	Asset	Liability	Owner's Capital	Owner's Withdrawals	Revenue	Expense		Debit	Credit
a.									
b.									
c.									
d.									
e.									
f.									
g.									
h.									
i.									
j.									
k.									
l.									
m.									
n.									
o.									
p.									
q.									
r.									
s.									
t.									
u.									
v.									

Chapter 2, E 4.

a.

b.

c.

d.

e.

f.

g.

Cash		Repair Supplies		Repair Equipment
a. 4,300				
Bal.				

Accounts Payable		Sally Felipe, Capital		Sally Felipe, Withdrawals

Repair Fees Earned		Salaries Expense		Rent Expense

Chapter 2, E 6.

Flagship Repair Service		
Trial Balance		
June 30, 20xx		

Chapter 2, E 7.

a.	
b.	
c.	
d.	
e.	
f.	
g.	
h.	

Chapter 2, E 8.

<table>
<tr><td colspan="3" align="center">**Collie Service Company**
Trial Balance
October 31, 20xx</td></tr>
<tr><td></td><td></td><td></td></tr>
<tr><td></td><td></td><td></td></tr>
<tr><td></td><td></td><td></td></tr>
<tr><td></td><td></td><td></td></tr>
<tr><td></td><td></td><td></td></tr>
<tr><td></td><td></td><td></td></tr>
<tr><td></td><td></td><td></td></tr>
<tr><td></td><td></td><td></td></tr>
<tr><td></td><td></td><td></td></tr>
<tr><td></td><td></td><td></td></tr>
<tr><td></td><td></td><td></td></tr>
</table>

Chapter 2, E 9.

a.	
b.	
c.	
d.	

Chapter 2, E 10.

La Pietro Services
Trial Balance
September 30, 20xx

Chapter 2, E 11.

Zigler Construction Company
Trial Balance
November 30, 20xx

Cash		

a.

b.

c.

d.

e.

f.

Chapter 2, E 13.

	General Journal				Page 10
Date	Description	Post. Ref.	Debit	Credit
20xx				
Dec. 14				
28				

General Ledger

Cash — Account No. 111

Date		Item	Post. Ref.	Debit	Credit	Balance Debit	Balance Credit
20xx							
Dec.	13	Balance				8,000	
	14						
	28						

Equipment — Account No. 144

Date		Item	Post. Ref.	Debit	Credit	Balance Debit	Balance Credit
20xx							
Dec.	14						

Accounts Payable — Account No. 212

Date		Item	Post. Ref.	Debit	Credit	Balance Debit	Balance Credit
20xx							
Dec.	14						
	28						

Chapter 2, P 1.

		Debit	Credit
a.			
b.			
c.			
d.			
e.			
f.			
g.			
h.			
i.			
j.			
k.			
l.			
m.			
n.			

1. T accounts set up
2. Transactions recorded in the accounts

Cash		Accounts Receivable		Software
a. 9,200				
Bal.				

Furniture		Microcomputers		Accounts Payable

Diane Pastore, Capital		Diane Pastore, Withdrawals		Tuition Revenue

Wages Expense		Utilities Expense		Rent Expense

Advertising Expense

3. Trial balance prepared

Pastore Training Center
Trial Balance
(Current Date)

4. Cash flow effects discussed

1. **Transactions entered in the general journal**

		General Journal			Page 1
Date		**Description**	**Post. Ref.**	**Debit**	**Credit**
20xx					
Mar.	1				
	2				
	3				
	4				
	5				
	8				
	10				
	15				
	16				
	21				
	24				

General Journal

Date		Description	Post. Ref.	Debit	Credit
20xx					
Mar.	25				
	29				
	30				
	31				

2. Ledger accounts set up and journal entries posted

Cash

Account No. 111

Date		Item	Post. Ref.	Debit	Credit	Balance Debit	Balance Credit
20xx							
Mar.	1		J1	17,000		17,000	
	2						
	5						
	8						
	15						
	21						
	24						
	25						
	29						
	30						
	31						

Accounts Receivable — Account No. 113

Date	Item	Post. Ref.	Debit	Credit	Balance Debit	Balance Credit
20xx						
Mar. 16						
29						

Photography Supplies — Account No. 115

Date	Item	Post. Ref.	Debit	Credit	Balance Debit	Balance Credit
20xx						
Mar. 10						

Prepaid Rent — Account No. 116

Date	Item	Post. Ref.	Debit	Credit	Balance Debit	Balance Credit
20xx						
Mar. 2						

Photography Equipment — Account No. 141

Date	Item	Post. Ref.	Debit	Credit	Balance Debit	Balance Credit
20xx						
Mar. 3						
8						

Office Equipment — Account No. 143

Date	Item	Post. Ref.	Debit	Credit	Balance Debit	Balance Credit
20xx						
Mar. 5						

Accounts Payable — Account No. 211

Date	Item	Post. Ref.	Debit	Credit	Balance Debit	Balance Credit
20xx						
Mar. 10						
21						

Chapter 2, P 3. (Continued)

Vic Kostro, Capital   Account No. 311

Date		Item	Post. Ref.	Debit	Credit	Balance Debit	Balance Credit
20xx							
Mar.	1		J1		17,000		17,000
	3						

Vic Kostro, Withdrawals   Account No. 312

Date		Item	Post. Ref.	Debit	Credit	Balance Debit	Balance Credit
20xx							
Mar.	31						

Portrait Revenue   Account No. 411

Date		Item	Post. Ref.	Debit	Credit	Balance Debit	Balance Credit
20xx							
Mar.	15						
	16						

Wages Expense   Account No. 511

Date		Item	Post. Ref.	Debit	Credit	Balance Debit	Balance Credit
20xx							
Mar.	30						

Utilities Expense   Account No. 512

Date		Item	Post. Ref.	Debit	Credit	Balance Debit	Balance Credit
20xx							
Mar.	24						

Telephone Expense   Account No. 513

Date		Item	Post. Ref.	Debit	Credit	Balance Debit	Balance Credit
20xx							
Mar.	25						

3. **Trial balance prepared**

Kostro Portrait Studio		
Trial Balance		
March 31, 20xx		

Chapter 2, P 4.

1. Transactions entered in journal form

20xx					
June	2	Cash		7,200	
		Hassan Rahim, Capital			7,200
		Owner's investment			
	3				
	4				
	5				
	6				
	8				
	9				
	10				
	13				
	16				
	17				

20xx June	18					
	20					
	22					
	23					
	25					
	27					
	29					
	30					

Chapter 2, P 4. (Continued)

2. T accounts set up and entries posted from the journal

Cash

6/2	7,200		
Bal.			

Accounts Receivable

Supplies

Shed

Bicycles

Accounts Payable

Hassan Rahim, Capital

Hassan Rahim, Withdrawals

Rental Revenue

Wages Expense

Maintenance Expense

Repair Expense

Concession Fee Expense

3. **Trial balance prepared**

Rahim Rentals
Trial Balance
June 30, 20xx

4. **Recognition and classification discussed**

Chapter 2, P 5.

1. Transactions entered in the general journal

		Description	Post. Ref.	Debit	Credit
	General Journal			Page 26
Date		Description	Post. Ref.	Debit	Credit
20xx					
May	1	Cash	111	4,200	
		Accounts Receivable	113		4,200
		Received payment from customers			
	2				
	3				
	5				
	6				
	7				
	9				
	14				
	16				

			General Journal			Page 27
Date			Description	Post. Ref.	Debit	Credit
20xx						
May	17					
	18					
	19					
	24					
	28					
	30					
	31					

Chapter 2, P 5. (Continued)

2. Ledger accounts set up
3. Amounts from April 30 trial balance entered
4. Entries from journal posted to ledger accounts

Cash — Account No. 111

Date		Item	Post. Ref.	Debit	Credit	Balance Debit	Balance Credit
20xx							
Apr.	30	Balance				13,300	
May	1		J26	4,200		17,500	
	2						
	3						
	7						
	9						
	14						
	17						
	18						
	24						
	28						
	31						

Accounts Receivable — Account No. 113

Date		Item	Post. Ref.	Debit	Credit	Balance Debit	Balance Credit
20xx							
Apr.	30	Balance				9,400	
May	1						
	6						
	30						

Supplies — Account No. 115

Date		Item	Post. Ref.	Debit	Credit	Balance Debit	Balance Credit
20xx							
Apr.	30						
May	5						
	19						

Prepaid Insurance — Account No. 116

Date		Item	Post. Ref.	Debit	Credit	Balance Debit	Balance Credit
20xx							
Apr.	30						
May	3						

Equipment — Account No. 141

Date		Item	Post. Ref.	Debit	Credit	Balance Debit	Balance Credit
20xx							
Apr.	30	Balance				7,800	
May	18						

Accounts Payable — Account No. 211

Date		Item	Post. Ref.	Debit	Credit	Balance Debit	Balance Credit
20xx							
Apr.	30	Balance					5,300
May	2						
	5						
	19						
	28						

Dennis Kinsella, Capital — Account No. 311

Date		Item	Post. Ref.	Debit	Credit	Balance Debit	Balance Credit
20xx							
Apr.	30	Balance					21,160

Dennis Kinsella, Withdrawals — Account No. 312

Date		Item	Post. Ref.	Debit	Credit	Balance Debit	Balance Credit
20xx							
Apr.	30						
May	24						

Security Services Revenue — Account No. 411

Date		Item	Post. Ref.	Debit	Credit	Balance Debit	Balance Credit
20xx							
Apr.	30						
May	6						
	9						
	30						

Wages Expense   Account No. 512

Date		Item	Post. Ref.	Debit	Credit	Balance Debit	Balance Credit
20xx							
Apr.	30						
May	14						
	31						

Rent Expense   Account No. 513

Date		Item	Post. Ref.	Debit	Credit	Balance Debit	Balance Credit
20xx							
Apr.	30	Balance				3,200	
May	7						

Utilities Expense   Account No. 514

Date		Item	Post. Ref.	Debit	Credit	Balance Debit	Balance Credit
20xx							
Apr.	30						
May	17						

5.   Trial balance prepared

Delta Security Service
Trial Balance
May 31, 20xx

Cash		$ 6,640	

		Debit	Credit
a.			
b.			
c.			
d.			
e.			
f.			
g.			
h.			
i.			
j.			
k.			
l.			
m.			
n.			

1. Transactions entered in journal form

20xx					
June	3				
	5				
	7				
	8				
	10				
	11				
	12				
	13				
	14				

Chapter 2, P 7. (Continued)

20xx					
June	16				
	18				
	19				
	20				
	21				
	23				
	24				
	25				
	26				
	28				
	29				

2. T accounts set up and entries posted from the journal

Cash

6/3	14,200		

Accounts Receivable

Supplies

Prepaid Insurance

Equipment

Truck

Bal.

Notes Payable

Accounts Payable

Tim Sauk, Capital

Tim Sauk, Withdrawals

Painting Fees Earned

Wages Expense

Telephone Expense

Truck Expense

3.   Trial balance prepared

Sauk Painting Service			
Trial Balance			
June 30, 20xx			

4.   Recognition and classification discussed

Chapter 2, P 8.

1. Transactions entered in the general journal

		General Journal			Page 11
Date		**Description**	**Post. Ref.**	**Debit**	**Credit**
20xx					
Aug.	1	Accounts Payable	212	140	
		Cash	111		140
		Paid for supplies purchased last month			
	2				
	3				
	5				
	7				
	8				
	9				
	12				
	13				

		General Journal			Page 12
Date		Description	Post. Ref.	Debit	Credit
20xx					
Aug.	14				
	16				
	19				
	20				
	23				
	25				
	27				
	29				

Chapter 2, P 8. (Continued)

2. **Ledger accounts set up**
3. **Amounts from July 31 trial balance entered**
4. **Entries from journal posted to ledger accounts**

Cash   **Account No. 111**

Date		Item	Post. Ref.	Debit	Credit	Balance Debit	Balance Credit
20xx							
July	31	Balance				3,100	
Aug.	1		J11		140	2,960	
	3						
	7						
	13						
	14						
	16						
	19						
	25						
	27						
	29						

Accounts Receivable   **Account No. 113**

Date		Item	Post. Ref.	Debit	Credit	Balance Debit	Balance Credit
20xx							
July	31						
Aug.	2						
	13						
	20						
	25						

Supplies   **Account No. 115**

Date		Item	Post. Ref.	Debit	Credit	Balance Debit	Balance Credit
20xx							
July	31						
Aug.	5						

Chapter 2, P 8. (Continued)

Prepaid Insurance — Account No. 116

Date		Item	Post. Ref.	Debit	Credit	Balance Debit	Balance Credit
20xx							
July	31						

Equipment — Account No. 141

Date		Item	Post. Ref.	Debit	Credit	Balance Debit	Balance Credit
20xx							
July	31						
Aug.	8						
	12						
	23						

Notes Payable — Account No. 211

Date		Item	Post. Ref.	Debit	Credit	Balance Debit	Balance Credit
20xx							
July	31	Balance					3,000
Aug.	29						

Accounts Payable — Account No. 212

Date		Item	Post. Ref.	Debit	Credit	Balance Debit	Balance Credit
20xx							
July	31						
Aug.	1						
	5						
	8						
	9						
	12						
	14						
	19						

Lou Jacobson, Capital — Account No. 311

Date		Item	Post. Ref.	Debit	Credit	Balance Debit	Balance Credit
20xx							
July	31						
Aug.	23						

Chapter 2, P 8. (Continued)

Lou Jacobson, Withdrawals — Account No. 312

Date		Item	Post. Ref.	Debit	Credit	Balance Debit	Balance Credit
20xx							
July	31						
Aug.	16						

Service Revenue — Account No. 411

Date		Item	Post. Ref.	Debit	Credit	Balance Debit	Balance Credit
20xx							
July	31						
Aug.	2						
	7						
	20						

Lease Expense — Account No. 511

Date		Item	Post. Ref.	Debit	Credit	Balance Debit	Balance Credit
20xx							
July	31	Balance				290	
Aug.	3						

Truck Expense — Account No. 512

Date		Item	Post. Ref.	Debit	Credit	Balance Debit	Balance Credit
20xx							
July	31						
Aug.	9						
	27						

5. Trial balance prepared

Lou's Landscaping Service
Trial Balance
August 31, 20xx

Chapter 2, SD 5.

1. June transactions recorded in journal form

2. Entries set up in T accounts

Cash	Accounts Receivable	Prepaid Rent
23,000		

Bal.

Truck	Office Equipment	Repair Tools

Accounts Payable	Unearned Revenue	Loan Payable

Truck Loan Payable	Ben Obi, Capital	Repair Revenue

Wages Expense	Utilities Expense	Interest Expense

Legal Expense

3. **Trial balance prepared**

Obi Repairs Company
Trial Balance
June 30, 20xx

4. **Information in trial balance evaluated**

Chapter 2, FRA 1.

1. Accounts classified

2. Transactions recorded in journal form

a.				
b.				
c.				

Chapter 2, FRA 2.

(Numbers are in millions of yen)

(Numbers are in millions)						
Cash and Cash Equivalents						
Jan.	29		584			
b.			35			
			619			
Bal.						

Accounts and Other Receivables					

Prepaid Expenses and Other Current Assets					

Accounts Payable					

Income Taxes Payable					

Chapter 3, SE 1.

1.
2.
3.
4.

Chapter 3, SE 2.

Dec.	31						
			To record insurance expired during the year				
				+	−	=	

Chapter 3, SE 3.

Dec.	31						
			To record supplies used during the year				
				+	−	=	

Chapter 3, SE 4.

Mar.	31				

Balance Sheet Presentation:

Chapter 3, SE 5.

June	30							
			To record wages accrued at the end of June					
			(	÷	)	x	=	

Chapter 3, SE 6.

Aug.	31				

Chapter 3, SE 7.

Heller Company
Income Statement
For the Month Ended December 31, 20x3

Revenues		
Expenses		
Net Income		

Chapter 3, SE 8.

Heller Company
Statement of Owner's Equity
For the Month Ended December 31, 20x3

Chapter 3, SE 9.

Chapter 3, SE 10.

77

Chapter 3, E 1.

1.	b.	4.	d a
2.	a d	5.	f
3.	e	6.	c

Chapter 3, E 2.

20x3					
Dec.	31				

Chapter 3, E 3.

1.

To record expired insurance

_ =

2.

Chapter 3, E 4.

1. Amounts indicated by the question marks are in italics

	a	b	c	d
Supplies on hand, October 1				$1,338
+ Supplies purchased during the month		1,461		
= Total supplies available				
− Supplies consumed during the month			471	
= Supplies on hand, October 31				

2. Adjusting entry for Column *a*

Oct. 31

Chapter 3, E 5.

1. July 31

To accrue salaries owed but not yet paid at month end

÷ = per day

X workdays (Monday and Tuesday) expired =

2. Aug. 3

Chapter 3, E 6.

1.   Royalty expense and royalty income calculated

January to June, 20x3 (payment on November 1)			
July to December, 20x3 (x percent)			
20x3 royalty expense and royalty income			

2.   Adjusting entries recorded

In Ninevah Systems Company's records:

20x3					
Dec.	31				

In Uruk Company's records:

20x3					
Dec.	31				

1.	Office Supplies Expense		428	
	Office Supplies			428
	To record supplies consumed			
	during period			
	Beginning balance	$168		
	+ **Purchases**	$830		
	= **Total available**	$998		
	− **Ending balance**	$570		
	Supplies consumed	$428		
2.				
	Depreciation expense	$4,260		
	Accumulated depreciation			$4,260
3.				
	Property Taxes Expense		$1,750	
	Property Taxes Payable			$1,750
4.				
	Interest Receivable		$1,700	
	Interest Revenue			1700
5.				
	Unearned revenue		$60000	
	~~Provided $600 of services/earned revenue~~			~~$600~~
	Service revenue			$600
6.				
	A/R		$400	
	Service Revenue			$400

Chapter 3, E 8.

1. Entries recorded

Apr.	1			
Dec.	31			
		To recognize nine months' fees earned		
		(÷ months)		
		x months =		

2.

Chapter 3, E 9.

Musket Custodial Services
Income Statement
For the Month Ended August 31, 20xx

Revenues		
Expenses		
Net Income		

Musket Custodial Services
Statement of Owner's Equity
For the Month Ended August 31, 20xx

Musket Custodial Services
Balance Sheet
August 31, 20xx

Assets

Liabilities

Owner's Equity

Chapter 3, E 10.

Insurance Expense:

Wages Expense:

Fees Earned:

Chapter 3, E 11.

Reported subscription revenue		
Less:		

Chapter 3, E 12.

1.	**Cash paid for rent during the year:**	
2.	**Cash paid for interest during the year:**	
3.	**Cash paid for salaries during the year:**	

	Balance Sheet Account	Amount of Adjustment (+ or −)	Balance after Adjustment	Income Statement Account	Amount of Adjustment (+ or −)	Balance after Adjustment
a.	Office Supplies	− 1,540	266	Office Supplies Expense	+ 1,540	266
b.	Prepaid Rent	+ 1,200	1,400	Rent Expense	+ 1,200	400
c.	Accumulated Depreciation, Equipment	+ 416	416	Depreciation Expense, Equipment	+ 416	416
d.	Unearned Answering Service Revenue	+ 296	1,480	Answering Service Revenue	+ 296	1480
e.	Wages Payable	+ 160	160	Wages Expense	+ 1,600	3960

86

a.	May	31					
			To record supplies used				
				+	−	=	
b.		31					
			To record expired insurance				
			[(÷ months)				
			x months]				
			[(÷ months)				
			x months]				
c.		31					
d.		31					
			To record service revenue earned on services collected in advance				
			(÷ months)				
			x months =				
e.		31					
f.		31					
g.		31					
			To record accrued salaries				
			(÷ days)				
			x days =				
h.		31					

Chapter 3, P 3.

1. **T accounts set up and balances entered**
2. **Adjusting entries posted to the accounts**

Cash			
Bal.	16,500		

Accounts Receivable			

Fees Receivable			

Office Supplies			

Prepaid Rent			

Office Equipment			

Accumulated Depreciation, Office Equipment			

Accounts Payable			

Notes Payable			

Interest Payable			

Salaries Payable			

Unearned Fees			

Sandy Chee, Capital			

Sandy Chee, Withdrawals			

Fees Revenue			

Salaries Expense			

Rent Expense			

Utilities Expense			

Office Supplies Expense			

Depreciation Expense, Office Equipment			

Interest Expense			

3.   Adjusted trial balance prepared

Fleet Relay Services		
Adjusted Trial Balance		
December 31, 20xx		

Chapter 3, P 4.

1.	T accounts set up and balances entered
2.	Adjusting entries posted to the accounts

(handwritten margin calculations, left side:)
```
2 7 10
8 8 2
 3 7
 348

     31.6
12 ) 380
    36
    20
   -12
    80
   -72
    80
```

Cash			Accounts Receivable			Fees Receivable		
Bal.	762		bal	914				

Prepaid Insurance			Prepaid Rent			Cleaning Supplies		
	380		31.6≈32	706		100	4,396		117
bal.	348						bal	1,379	

Cleaning Equipment			Accumulated Depreciation, Cleaning Equipment			Truck		
	1,740						3,500	

Accumulated Depreciation, Truck			Accounts Payable			Wages Payable		
					170			

Unearned Janitorial Fees			Mike Podgorney, Capital			Mike Podgorney, Withdrawals		
		480			7,095		3,000	

Janitorial Fees			Wages Expense			Rent Expense		
		7,487		2,400				

Gas, Oil, and Other Truck Expenses			Insurance Expense			Cleaning Supplies Expense		
	340							

Depreciation Expense, Cleaning Equipment			Depreciation Expense, Truck					

3. Adjusted trial balance, income statement, statement of owner's equity, and balance sheet prepared

Crescent Custodial Service Adjusted Trial Balance June 30, 20xx		

Crescent Custodial Service
Income Statement
For the Six Months Ended June 30, 20xx

Revenues		
Expenses		
Net Income		

Crescent Custodial Service
Statement of Owner's Equity
For the Six Months Ended June 30, 20xx

Add:		

Crescent Custodial Service
Balance Sheet
June 30, 20xx

Assets

Liabilities

Owner's Equity

1.   Adjusting entries recorded in the general journal

		General Journal			Page 53
Date		**Description**	**Post. Ref.**	**Debit**	**Credit**
20x2					
Oct.	**31**				
		To record supplies used			
		– =			
	31				
		To record expired rent for October			
		(÷ months)			
		x month			
	31				
		To record expired insurance			
		(÷ months)			
		x months			
	31				
	31				
	31				
		To record dance fees earned by October 31			
		x / =			

Chapter 3, P 5. (Continued)

2. **Ledger accounts opened and balances recorded**
3. **Adjusting entries posted from the general journal**

Cash   Account No. 111

Date		Item	Post. Ref.	Debit	Credit	Balance Debit	Balance Credit
20x2							
Oct.	31	Balance					

Accounts Receivable   Accounts Receivable

Date		Item	Post. Ref.	Debit	Credit	Balance Debit	Balance Credit
20x2							
Oct.	31						

Supplies   Account No. 115

Date		Item	Post. Ref.	Debit	Credit	Balance Debit	Balance Credit
20x2							
Oct.	31						
	31						

Prepaid Rent   Account No. 116

Date		Item	Post. Ref.	Debit	Credit	Balance Debit	Balance Credit
20x2							
Oct.	31						
	31						

Prepaid Insurance   Account No. 117

Date		Item	Post. Ref.	Debit	Credit	Balance Debit	Balance Credit
20x2							
Oct.	31						
	31						

Equipment
Account No. 141

Date		Item	Post. Ref.	Debit	Credit	Balance Debit	Balance Credit
20x2							
Oct.	31						

Accumulated Depreciation, Equipment
Account No. 142

Date		Item	Post. Ref.	Debit	Credit	Balance Debit	Balance Credit
20x2							
Oct.	31						
	31						

Accounts Payable
Account No. 211

Date		Item	Post. Ref.	Debit	Credit	Balance Debit	Balance Credit
20x2							
Oct.	31						

Wages Payable
Account No. 212

Date		Item	Post. Ref.	Debit	Credit	Balance Debit	Balance Credit
20x2							
Oct.	31						

Unearned Dance Fees
Account No. 213

Date		Item	Post. Ref.	Debit	Credit	Balance Debit	Balance Credit
20x2							
Oct.	31						
	31						

Midge Bronson, Capital
Account No. 311

Date		Item	Post. Ref.	Debit	Credit	Balance Debit	Balance Credit
20x3							
Oct.	31						

Chapter 3, P 5. (Continued)

Midge Bronson, Withdrawals — Account No. 312

Date		Item	Post. Ref.	Debit	Credit	Balance Debit	Balance Credit
20x2							
Oct.	31						

Dance Fees — Account No. 411

Date		Item	Post. Ref.	Debit	Credit	Balance Debit	Balance Credit
20x2							
Oct.	31						
	31						

Wages Expense — Account No. 511

Date		Item	Post. Ref.	Debit	Credit	Balance Debit	Balance Credit
20x2							
Oct.	31						
	31						

Rent Expense — Account No. 512

Date		Item	Post. Ref.	Debit	Credit	Balance Debit	Balance Credit
20x2							
Oct.	31						
	31						

Supplies Expense — Account No. 513

Date		Item	Post. Ref.	Debit	Credit	Balance Debit	Balance Credit
20x2							
Oct.	31						

Insurance Expense — Account No. 514

Date		Item	Post. Ref.	Debit	Credit	Balance Debit	Balance Credit
20x2							
Oct.	31						

Chapter 3, P 5. (Continued)

Utilities Expense — Account No. 515

Date		Item	Post. Ref.	Debit	Credit	Balance Debit	Balance Credit
20x2							
Oct.	31						

Depreciation Expense, Equipment — Account No. 516

Date		Item	Post. Ref.	Debit	Credit	Balance Debit	Balance Credit
20x2							
Oct.	31						

Chapter 3, P 5. (Continued)

4. Adjusted trial balance, income statement, statement of owner's equity, and balance sheet prepared

New Wave Dance Studio Adjusted Trial Balance October 31, 20x2		

New Wave Dance Studio
Income Statement
For the Year Ended October 31, 20x2

Revenues		
Expenses		
Net Income		

New Wave Dance Studio
Statement of Owner's Equity
For the Year Ended October 31, 20x2

New Wave Dance Studio		
Balance Sheet		
October 31, 20x2		
Assets		
Liabilities		
Owner's Equity		

	Balance Sheet Account	Amount of Adjustment (+ or −)	Balance after Adjustment	Income Statement Account	Amount of Adjustment (+ or −)	Balance after Adjustment
a.	Prepaid Insurance	− $1,360	$ 340	Insurance Expense	+ $1,360	$ 1,360
b.	Cleaning Supplies			Supplies Expense		
c.	Accumulated Depreciation, Building			Depreciation Expense, Building		
d.	Interest Payable			Interest Expense		
e.	Unearned Dry Cleaning Revenue			Dry Cleaning Revenue		
f.	Wages Payable			Wages Expense		

a.	June	30				
b.		30				
			To record accrued salaries			
			(	÷	days) x	days
			=			
c.						
d.		30				
			To record supplies used			
			+	−		
			=			
e.		30				
			To record expired insurance			
			[(	÷	months)	
			x	months]		
			[(	÷	months)	
			x	months]		
f.		30				
g.		30				
			To record service revenue earned on services collected in advance			
			(	÷	months) x	month
			=			
h.		30				

Chapter 3, P 8.

1. **T accounts set up and balances entered**
2. **Adjusting entries posted to the accounts**

Cash				Accounts Receivable				Fees Receivable		
Bal.	12,786									

Office Supplies				Prepaid Rent				Office Equipment		

Accumulated Depreciation, Office Equipment				Accounts Payable				Notes Payable		

Interest Payable				Salaries Payable				Unearned Fees		

Nils Haveczech, Capital				Nils Haveczech, Withdrawals				Fees Revenue		

Salaries Expense				Utilities Expense				Rent Expense		

Office Supplies Expense				Depreciation Expense, Office Equipment				Interest Expense		

3.   Adjusted trial balance prepared

Alpha Advisory Company
Adjusted Trial Balance
March 31, 20x3

1. Adjusting entries prepared

a.						
		Recording of supplies used				
			−		=	
b.						
c.						
d.						
		Recognition of subscriptions fulfilled				
			x	1/3	=	

2. **Financial statement amounts recast**

	Before	Adjustments				After
Revenues				(d)		
Expenses		(a)				
		(b)				
		(c)				
Net Income						
				(a)		
Total Assets				(b)		
Liabilities		(d)		(c)		
Owner's Equity						
Total Liabilities and Owner's Equity						

3. **Results discussed**

1. **Film and television costs defined**

2. **Journal entry made**

3. **Film and Television Program Expense recorded**

Adjusting Entry

4. **Matching rule discussed**

Chapter 3, FRA 2.

1. Current liabilities identified

The following current liabilities definitely would have arisen from adjusting entries:

Total	

Part of the following current liabilities probably arose from adjusting entries:

Total	

The following accounts probably did not arise from adjusting entries:

Total	

2. Effects of adjustments explained

Chapter 4, SE 1.

Chapter 4, SE 2.

Dec.	31			

Chapter 4, SE 3.

Dec.	31			

Chapter 4, SE 4.

Dec.	31			

Chapter 4, SE 5.

Dec.	31			

Chapter 4, SE 6.

R. Richards, Capital			R. Richards, Withdrawals		
Dec. 31	800				
		Bal.			

Income Summary			Patient Services Revenues		

Laboratory Fees Revenues			Rent Expense		

Wages Expense			Other Expenses		

Chapter 4, SE 7.

Apr.	1			

Chapter 4, SE 8.

Salaries Payable			Salaries Expense		
Apr. 1	360				
		Bal.			

Chapter 4, SE 9.

Dec.	31					
	31					
	31					
	31					

Chapter 4, E 1.

Dec.	31					
	31					
	31					
	31					

Chapter 4, E 2.

1. Appropriateness of reversing entry explained

2. Reversing entry prepared

20xx				
Oct.	1			

3. Entry for payment of wages

20xx				
Oct.	3			

Ali Realty
Trial Balance
June 30, 20x3

Chapter 4, E 4.

1. Trial balance amounts entered on the work sheet
2. Work sheet completed

For the Month Ended March 31, 20xx

Account Name	Trial Balance Debit	Trial Balance Credit	Adjustments Debit	Adjustments Credit	Adjusted Trial Balance Debit	Adjusted Trial Balance Credit	Income Statement Debit	Income Statement Credit	Balance Sheet Debit	Balance Sheet Credit
Prepaid Insurance				(a)						

Axel's Barber Shop
Statement of Owner's Equity
For the Year Ended December 31, 20x1

Chapter 4, E 6.

1. Adjustments made

(a)

(b)

(c)

(d)

(e)

2. Balance sheet completed

Balance Sheet
Assets

Liabilities

Owner's Equity

Chapter 4, E 7.

1. Adjusting entries prepared

	20xx					
(a)	June	30				
(b)		30				
(c)		30				
(d)		30				
(e)		30				

2. Appropriate reversing entries prepared

	20xx					
(e)	July	1				

Chapter 4, E 8.

20xx						
Dec.	31					
	31					
	31					
			Closed the Income Summary account			
			−	=		
	31					

Chapter 4, P 1.

1. T accounts opened and balances entered
2. Closing entries entered in T accounts

Emma Glorry, Capital

(d)	Dec.	31	12,000				

Emma Glorry, Withdrawals

Income Summary

Revenues

Wages Expense

Advertising Expense

Maintenance Expense

Chapter 4, P 1. (Continued)

Supplies Expense

Insurance Expense

Depreciation Expense, Building

Depreciation Expense, Equipment

Utilities Expense

Miscellaneous Expense

Property Taxes Expense

Chapter 4, P 1. (Continued)

3. Income statement, statement of owner's equity, and balance sheet prepared

<table>
<tr><td colspan="3" align="center">Glorry Bowling Lanes
Income Statement
For the Year Ended December 31, 20x3</td></tr>
<tr><td>Revenues</td><td></td><td></td></tr>
<tr><td>Expenses</td><td></td><td></td></tr>
<tr><td></td><td></td><td></td></tr>
<tr><td></td><td></td><td></td></tr>
<tr><td></td><td></td><td></td></tr>
<tr><td></td><td></td><td></td></tr>
<tr><td></td><td></td><td></td></tr>
<tr><td></td><td></td><td></td></tr>
<tr><td></td><td></td><td></td></tr>
<tr><td></td><td></td><td></td></tr>
<tr><td></td><td></td><td></td></tr>
<tr><td></td><td></td><td></td></tr>
<tr><td>Net Income</td><td></td><td></td></tr>
</table>

<table>
<tr><td colspan="3" align="center">Glorry Bowling Lanes
Statement of Owner's Equity
For the Year Ended December 31, 20x3</td></tr>
<tr><td></td><td></td><td></td></tr>
<tr><td></td><td></td><td></td></tr>
<tr><td></td><td></td><td></td></tr>
<tr><td></td><td></td><td></td></tr>
<tr><td></td><td></td><td></td></tr>
</table>

Glorry Bowling Lanes
Balance Sheet
December 31, 20x3

Assets

Liabilities

Owner's Equity

Chapter 4, P 2.

1. Income statement, statement of owner's equity, and balance sheet prepared

Pines Recreational Park
Income Statement
For the Year Ended November 30, 20x3

Revenues		
Campsite Rentals		88,200
Expenses		
Wages Expense	23,850	
Insurance Expense	3,784	
Utilities Expense	1,800	
Supplies Expense	1,320	
Depreciation Expense	6,000	
		36,754
Net Income		51,446

Pines Recreational Park
Statement of Owner's Equity
For the Year Ended November 30, 20x3

Emmit Howes, Capital, December 1, 20x3		93,070
Net Income		51,446
Subtotal		144,516
Less Withdrawals		36,000
Emmit Howes, Capital, November 30, 20x3		108,516

Pines Recreational Park
Balance Sheet
November 30, 20x3

Assets

Cash		4,080
A/R		7,320
Supplies		228
Pre-paid Insurance		1,188
Land		30,000
Less Building	91,800	
→ Accumulated Dep, Building	21,000	70800
Total Assets		113,616

Liabilities

A/P		3,450
Wages Payable		1,650
Total liabilities		5,100

Owner's Equity

Emmit Howes, Capital		108,516
Total Liabilities and Owner's Equity		113,616

2. Closing entries prepared

20x3					
November	30	campsite Rentals		88,200	
		Income Summary			88,200
		To close the revenue account			
	30	Income Summary		36,754	
		Wages Expense			23,850
		Insurance Expense			3,784
		Utilities Expense			1,800
		Supplies Expense			1,320
		Dep. Exp., Building			6,000
		To close the expense accounts			
	30	Income Summary		51,446	
		Emmit Howes, Capital			51,446
		To close the income summary account			
	30	Emmit Howes, Capital		36,000	
		Emmit Howes, Withdrawals			36,000
		To close the withdrawals account			

3. Reversing entry prepared

20x3					
December	1	Wages payable		1,650	
		Wages Expense			1,650
		To record the reversing entry for wages accrued			

Chapter 4, P 3.

1.	Journal entries for May prepared
3.	Adjusting entries for May prepared
6.	Closing entries for May prepared

	General Journal			Page 1
Date	**Description**	**Post. Ref.**	**Debit**	**Credit**
20xx				
May 1				
1				
1				
2				
5				
14				
15				
20				

		General Journal			Page 2
Date		Description	Post. Ref.	Debit	Credit
20xx					
May	**29**				
	31				
		Adjusting entries:			
May	**31**				
	31				
	31				

		General Journal	Post. Ref.	Debit	Credit		Page 3
Date		Description					
		<u>Closing entries:</u>					
20xx							
May	31						
	31						
	31						
	31						

4. **May adjusted trial balance prepared**

Springer Repair Store
Adjusted Trial Balance
May 31, 20xx

5. **May income statement, statement of owner's equity, and balance sheet prepared**

Springer Repair Store
Income Statement
For the Month Ended May 31, 20xx

Revenues		
Expenses		
Net Income		

Springer Repair Store
Statement of Owner's Equity
For the Month Ended May 31, 20xx

Add:		

Springer Repair Store
Balance Sheet
May 31, 20xx

Assets

Liabilities

Owner's Equity

7. **May post-closing trial balance prepared**

Springer Repair Store
Post-Closing Trial Balance
May 31, 20xx

Chapter 4, P 3. (Continued)

8.	Journal entries for June prepared
9.	Adjusting entries for June prepared
12.	Closing entries for June prepared

		General Journal			Page 4

Date		Description	Post. Ref.	Debit	Credit
20xx					
June	1				
	1				
	9				
	15				
	18				
	19				
	28				
	30				

Date		Description	Post. Ref.	Debit	Credit
		General Journal			**Page 5**
		Adjusting entries:			
20xx					
June	30				
	30				
	30				
		Closing entries:			
June	30				
	30				
	30				
	30				

Chapter 4, P 3. (Continued)

2.	Accounts opened and May entries posted
3.	Adjusting entries for May posted
6.	Closing entries for May posted
8.	June entries posted
9.	Adjusting entries for June posted
12.	Closing entries for June posted

Cash — Account No. 111

Date		Item	Post. Ref.	Debit	Credit	Balance Debit	Balance Credit
20xx							
May	1						
	1						
	1						
	2						
	14						
	15						
	20						
	29						
	31						
June	1						
	1						
	15						
	18						
	19						
	28						
	30						

Prepaid Insurance — Account No. 117

Date		Item	Post. Ref.	Debit	Credit	Balance Debit	Balance Credit
20xx							
May	1						
	31						
June	30						

Repair Supplies — Account No. 119

Date		Item	Post. Ref.	Debit	Credit	Balance Debit	Balance Credit
20xx							
May	5						
	31						
June	6						
	30						

Repair Equipment — Account No. 144

Date		Item	Post. Ref.	Debit	Credit	Balance Debit	Balance Credit
20xx							
May	2						

Accumulated Depreciation, Repair Equipment — Account No. 145

Date		Item	Post. Ref.	Debit	Credit	Balance Debit	Balance Credit
20xx							
May	31						
June	30						

Accounts Payable — Account No. 212

Date		Item	Post. Ref.	Debit	Credit	Balance Debit	Balance Credit
20xx							
May	2						
	5						
	20						
June	1						
	9						
	19						

Will Springer, Capital   Account No. 311

Date		Item	Post. Ref.	Debit	Credit	Balance Debit	Credit
20xx							
May	1						
	31						
	31						
June	30						
	30						

Will Springer, Withdrawals   Account No. 312

Date		Item	Post. Ref.	Debit	Credit	Balance Debit	Credit
20xx							
May	29						
	31						
June	28						
	30						

Income Summary   Account No. 313

Date		Item	Post. Ref.	Debit	Credit	Balance Debit	Credit
20xx							
May	31						
	31						
	31						
June	30						
	30						
	30						

Bicycle Repair Revenue — Account No. 411

Date		Item	Post. Ref.	Debit	Credit	Balance Debit	Balance Credit
20xx							
May	15						
	31						
	31						
June	15						
	30						
	30						

Store Rent Expense — Account No. 511

Date		Item	Post. Ref.	Debit	Credit	Balance Debit	Balance Credit
20xx							
May	1						
	31						
June	1						
	30						

Utilities Expense — Account No. 512

Date		Item	Post. Ref.	Debit	Credit	Balance Debit	Balance Credit
20xx							
May	14						
	31						
June	18						
	30						

Insurance Expense   Account No. 513

Date		Item	Post. Ref.	Debit	Credit	Balance Debit	Balance Credit
20xx							
May	31						
	31						
June	30						
	30						

Repair Supplies Expense   Account No. 514

Date		Item	Post. Ref.	Debit	Credit	Balance Debit	Balance Credit
20xx							
May	31						
	31						
June	30						
	30						

Depreciation Expense, Repair Equipment   Account No. 515

Date		Item	Post. Ref.	Debit	Credit	Balance Debit	Balance Credit
20xx							
May	31						
	31						
June	30						
	30						

10. | **June adjusted trial balance prepared**

Springer Repair Store
Adjusted Trial Balance
June 30, 20xx

11. **June income statement, statement of owner's equity, and balance sheet prepared**

Springer Repair Store
Income Statement
For the Month Ended June 30, 20xx

Revenues		
Expenses		
Net Income		

Springer Repair Store
Statement of Owner's Equity
For the Month Ended June 30, 20xx

Springer Repair Store
Balance Sheet
June 30, 20xx

Assets

Liabilities

Owner's Equity

13. **June post-closing trial balance prepared**

Springer Repair Store
Post-Closing Trial Balance
June 30, 20xx

1. Work sheet completed

Roman Patel, Consultant
Work Sheet
For the Year Ended December 31, 20x3

Account Name	Trial Balance		Adjustments		Adjusted Trial Balance		Income Statement		Balance Sheet	
	Debit	Credit	Debit	Credit	Debit	Credit	Debit	Credit	Debit	Credit
Cash										
Accounts Receivable										
Office Supplies										
Office Equipment										
Accumulated Depreciation, Office Equipment										
Accounts Payable										
Unearned Retainers										
Roman Patel, Capital										
Roman Patel, Withdrawals										
Consulting Fees										
Wages Expense										
Utilities Expense										
Rent Expense										
Office Supplies Expense										
Depreciation Expense, Office Equipment										
Consulting Fees Receivable										
Wages Payable										
Net Income										

2.   Income statement, statement of owner's equity, and balance sheet prepared

Roman Patel, Consultant
Income Statement
For the Year Ended December 31, 20x3

Revenues		
Expenses		
Net Income		

Roman Patel, Consultant
Statement of Owner's Equity
For the Year Ended December 31, 20x3

Roman Patel, Consultant
Balance Sheet
December 31, 20x3

Assets

Liabilities

Owner's Equity

		Chapter 4, P 4. (Continued)		
		3. Adjusting, closing, and reversing entries prepared		
		<u>Adjusting entries:</u>		
20x3				
Dec.	31			
	31			
	31			
	31			
	31			
		<u>Closing entries:</u>		
Dec.	31			

Chapter 4, P 4. (Continued)

20x3					
Dec.	31				
	31				
	31				
		Reversing entries:			
20x4					
Jan.	1				
	1				

Chapter 4, P 6.

1. **T accounts opened and balances entered**
2. **Closing entries entered in T accounts**

Bridget Lahey, Capital

(d)	June	30	108,000				

Bridget Lahey, Withdrawals

Income Summary

Revenues from Court Fees

Revenues from Locker Fees

Wages Expense

Maintenance Expense

Advertising Expense

Utilities Expense

Supplies Expense

Depreciation Expense, Building

Depreciation Expense, Equipment

Property Taxes Expense

Miscellaneous Expense

3. Income statement, statement of owner's equity, and balance sheet prepared

Palmetto Tennis Club Income Statement For the Year Ended June 30, 20x2		
Revenues		
Expenses		
Net Income		

Palmetto Tennis Club Statement of Owner's Equity For the Year Ended June 30, 20x2		

Palmetto Tennis Club
Balance Sheet
June 30, 20x2

Assets

Liabilities

Owner's Equity

1. Closing entries prepared

		Closing entries:		
20x4				
June	**30**			
	30			
	30			
	30			

2.   **Income statement, statement of owner's equity, and balance sheet prepared**

Quality Trailer Rental
Income Statement
For the Year Ended June 30, 20x4

Revenues		
Expenses		
Net Income		

Quality Trailer Rental
Statement of Owner's Equity
For the Year Ended June 30, 20x4

Chapter 4, P 7. (Continued)

Quality Trailer Rental		
Balance Sheet		
June 30, 20x4		
Assets		
Liabilities		
Owner's Equity		

1. Work sheet completed

Natchez Delivery Service—Work Sheet—For the Year Ended August 31, 20x2

Account Name	Trial Balance		Adjustments		Adjusted Trial Balance		Income Statement		Balance Sheet	
	Debit	Credit	Debit	Credit	Debit	Credit	Debit	Credit	Debit	Credit
Cash										
Accounts Receivable										
Prepaid Insurance										
Delivery Supplies										
Office Supplies										
Land										
Building										
Accumulated Depreciation, Building										
Trucks										
Accumulated Depreciation, Trucks										
Office Equipment										
Accumulated Depreciation, Office Equipment										
Accounts Payable										
Unearned Lockbox Fees										
Mortgage Payable										
Honore Natchez, Capital										
Honore Natchez, Withdrawals										
Delivery Services Revenue										
Lockbox Fees Earned										
Truck Drivers' Wages Expense										
Office Salaries Expense										
Gas, Oil, and Truck Repairs Expense										
Interest Expense										
Insurance Expense										
Delivery Supplies Expense										
Office Supplies Expense										
Depreciation Expense, Building										
Depreciation Expense, Trucks										
Depreciation Expense, Office Equipment										
Lockbox Fees Receivable										
Wages Payable										
Net Income										

2. **Income statement, statement of owner's equity, and balance sheet prepared**

Natchez Delivery Service Income Statement For the Year Ended December 31, 20x2		
Revenues		
Expenses		
Net Income		

Natchez Delivery Service Statement of Owner's Equity For the Year Ended December 31, 20x2		

Natchez Delivery Service
Balance Sheet
December 31, 20x2

Assets

Liabilities

Owner's Equity

3. Adjusting, closing, and reversing entries prepared

			Adjusting entries:		
20x2					
Dec.	31				
	31				
			Recorded delivery supplies used		
			− =		
	31				
			Recorded office supplies used		
			− =		
	31				
	31				
	31				
	31				
	31				

Chapter 4, P 8. (Continued)

20x2					
Dec.	31				
		Closing entries:			
Dec.	31				
	31				
	31				
	31				
		Reversing entries:			
20x3					
Jan.	1				
	1				

Chapter 4, SD 5.

1. Statement of cash receipts and expenditures prepared

Adele's Secretarial Service
Statement of Cash Receipts and Expenditures
For the Year Ended June 30, 20x4

Cash Receipts from Customers				a
Cash Expenditures				
Rent				
Supplies		b		
Other Expenses				
Owner's Withdrawals		c		
Total Cash Expenditures				
Increase in Cash				d

Explanations

a.

b.

c.

d.

Chapter 4, SD 5. (Continued)

2.	Memorandum explaining balance sheet changes and treatment of depreciation expense prepared

<u>**Memorandum**</u>

Date:	
To:	
From:	
Re:	

166

1. **Closing entries prepared**

(numbers are in thousands)

2.

Comprehensive Problem: Joan Miller Advertising Agency

1.	Reversing entries prepared and posted
2 and 3.	Transactions for February journalized and posted
7 and 8.	Adjusting and closing entries prepared and posted

		General Journal			Page 5
Date		Description	Post. Ref.	Debit	Credit
		Reversing entries			
20xx Feb.	1				
	1				
		Transactions for February			
	1				
	2				
	5				
	6				
	7				
	8				

Date		Description	Post. Ref.	Debit	Credit
20xx					
Feb.	9				
20xx					
Feb.	12				
	13				
	14				
	15				
	16				
	19				

Comprehensive Problem: Joan Miller Advertising Agency (Continued)

			General Journal			Page 7

Date			Description	Post. Ref.	Debit	Credit
20xx						
Feb.	20					
	21					
	22					
	23					
	26					
	27					
	28					
		Adjusting entries				
Feb.	28					

Date			Description	Post. Ref.	Debit	Credit
20xx						
Feb.	28					
	28					
			Recognized art supplies used			
			during the month			
			— | x | =			
	28					
			Recognized office supplies used			
			during the month			
			— | =			
	28					
	28					
	28					
	28					
	28					
			Accrued unrecorded wages			
			÷ | x | / | =			

		General Journal			Page 9
Date		Description	Post. Ref.	Debit	Credit
		Closing entries			
20xx					
Feb.	28				
	28				
	28				
	28				

Comprehensive Problem: Joan Miller Advertising Agency (Continued)

General Ledger

Cash						Account No. 111	
			Post.			Balance	
Date		Item	Ref.	Debit	Credit	Debit	Credit
20xx							
Jan.	1						
	2						
	4						
	5						
	8						
	9						
	10						
	12						
	15						
	26						
	29						
	31						
Feb.	1						
	2						
	6						
	9						
	12						
	13						
	14						
	15						
	16						
	19						
	21						
	22						
	23						
	26						
	28						

Accounts Receivable — Account No. 113

Date		Item	Post. Ref.	Debit	Credit	Balance Debit	Balance Credit
20xx							
Jan.	19						
Feb.	8						
	16						
	20						

Fees Receivable — Account No. 114

Date		Item	Post. Ref.	Debit	Credit	Balance Debit	Balance Credit
20xx							
Jan.	31	Adj. (i)					
Feb.	1	Reversing					
	28	Adj. (i)					

Art Supplies — Account No. 115

Date		Item	Post. Ref.	Debit	Credit	Balance Debit	Balance Credit
20xx							
Jan.	6						
	31						
Feb.	7						
	28						

Office Supplies — Account No. 116

Date		Item	Post. Ref.	Debit	Credit	Balance Debit	Balance Credit
20xx							
Jan.	6						
	31						
Feb.	6						
	28						

Prepaid Rent — Account No. 117

Date		Item	Post. Ref.	Debit	Credit	Balance Debit	Balance Credit
20xx							
Jan.	2						
	31						
Feb.	26						
	28						

Prepaid Insurance — Account No. 118

Date		Item	Post. Ref.	Debit	Credit	Balance Debit	Balance Credit
20xx							
Jan.	8						
	31						
Feb.	28						

Art Equipment — Account No. 144

Date		Item	Post. Ref.	Debit	Credit	Balance Debit	Balance Credit
20xx							
Jan.	4						
Feb.	5						

Accumulated Depreciation, Art Equipment — Account No. 145

Date		Item	Post. Ref.	Debit	Credit	Balance Debit	Balance Credit
20xx							
Jan.	31						
Feb.	28						

Office Equipment — Account No. 146

Date		Item	Post. Ref.	Debit	Credit	Balance Debit	Balance Credit
20xx							
Jan.	5						
Feb.	2						
	14						

Comprehensive Problem: Joan Miller Advertising Agency (Continued)

Accumulated Depreciation, Office Equipment   Account No. 147

Date		Item	Post. Ref.	Debit	Credit	Balance Debit	Balance Credit
20xx							
Jan.	31						
Feb.	28						

Accounts Payable   Account No. 212

Date		Item	Post. Ref.	Debit	Credit	Balance Debit	Balance Credit
20xx							
Jan.	5						
	6						
	9						
	30						
Feb.	7						
	12						
	14						
	19						
	27						

Unearned Art Fees   Account No. 213

Date		Item	Post. Ref.	Debit	Credit	Balance Debit	Balance Credit
20xx							
Jan.	15						
	31						
Feb.	13						
	28						

Comprehensive Problem: Joan Miller Advertising Agency (Continued)

Wages Payable — Account No. 214

Date		Item	Post. Ref.	Debit	Credit	Balance Debit	Balance Credit
20xx							
Jan.	31						
Feb.	1						
	28						

Joan Miller, Capital — Account No. 311

Date		Item	Post. Ref.	Debit	Credit	Balance Debit	Balance Credit
20xx							
Jan.	1						
	31						
	31						
Feb.	1						
	5						
	28						
	28						

Joan Miller, Withdrawals — Account No. 312

Date		Item	Post. Ref.	Debit	Credit	Balance Debit	Balance Credit
20xx							
Jan.	31						
	31						
Feb.	28						
	28						

Income Summary — Account No. 313

Date		Item	Post. Ref.	Debit	Credit	Balance Debit	Balance Credit
20xx							
Jan.	31						
	31						
	31						
Feb.	28						
	28						
	28						

Advertising Fees Earned

Account No. 411

Date		Item	Post. Ref.	Debit	Credit	Balance Debit	Balance Credit
20xx							
Jan.	10						
	19						
	31						
	31						
Feb.	1						
	8						
	15						
	20						
	28						
	28						

Art Fees Earned

Account No. 412

Date		Item	Post. Ref.	Debit	Credit	Balance Debit	Balance Credit
20xx							
Jan.	31						
	31						
Feb.	21						
	28						
	28						

Wages Expense

Account No. 511

Date		Item	Post. Ref.	Debit	Credit	Balance Debit	Balance Credit
20xx							
Jan.	12						
	26						
	31						
	31						
Feb.	1						
	9						
	23						
	28						
	28						

Comprehensive Problem: Joan Miller Advertising Agency (Continued)

Utilities Expense — Account No. 512

Date		Item	Post. Ref.	Debit	Credit	Balance Debit	Credit
20xx							
Jan.	29						
	31						
Feb.	22						
	28						

Telephone Expense — Account No. 513

Date		Item	Post. Ref.	Debit	Credit	Balance Debit	Credit
20xx							
Jan.	30						
	31						
Feb.	27						
	28						

Rent Expense — Account No. 514

Date		Item	Post. Ref.	Debit	Credit	Balance Debit	Credit
20xx							
Jan.	31						
	31						
Feb.	28						
	28						

Insurance Expense — Account No. 515

Date		Item	Post. Ref.	Debit	Credit	Balance Debit	Credit
20xx							
Jan.	31						
	31						
Feb.	28						
	28						

Comprehensive Problem: Joan Miller Advertising Agency (Continued)

Art Supplies Expense

Account No. 516

Date		Item	Post. Ref.	Debit	Credit	Balance Debit	Balance Credit
20xx							
Jan.	31						
	31						
Feb.	28						
	28						

Office Supplies Expense

Account No. 517

Date		Item	Post. Ref.	Debit	Credit	Balance Debit	Balance Credit
20xx							
Jan.	31						
	31						
Feb.	28						
	28						

Depreciation Expense, Art Equipment

Account No. 519

Date		Item	Post. Ref.	Debit	Credit	Balance Debit	Balance Credit
20xx							
Jan.	31						
	31						
Feb.	28						
	28						

Depreciation Expense, Office Equipment

Account No. 520

Date		Item	Post. Ref.	Debit	Credit	Balance Debit	Balance Credit
20xx							
Jan.	31						
	31						
Feb.	28						
	28						

Comprehensive Problem: Joan Miller Advertising Agency (Continued)

4 and 5.   Trial balance and work sheet prepared

Joan Miller Advertising Agency
Work Sheet
For the Month Ended February 28, 20xx

Account Name	Trial Balance		Adjustments		Adjusted Trial Balance		Income Statement		Balance Sheet	
	Debit	Credit	Debit	Credit	Debit	Credit	Debit	Credit	Debit	Credit
Cash										
Net Income										

181

6. Income statement, statement of owner's equity, and balance sheet prepared

Joan Miller Advertising Agency
Income Statement
For the Month Ended February 28, 20xx

Joan Miller Advertising Agency
Statement of Owner's Equity
For the Month Ended February 28, 20xx

Joan Miller Advertising Agency		
Balance Sheet		
February 28, 20xx		
Assets		
Liabilities		
Owner's Equity		

Comprehensive Problem: Joan Miller Advertising Agency (Continued)		
9. **Post-closing trial balance prepared**		

Joan Miller Advertising Agency Post-Closing Trial Balance February 28, 20xx		

Chapter 5, SE 1.

1.
2.
3.
4.

Chapter 5, SE 2.

Melchior Hardware
Income Statement
For the Month Ended February 28, 20xx

Net Sales		

Chapter 5, SE 3.

List price	
Less 40 percent	
Dealer price	
Shipping cost	
Cost of machine tool	
Less sales discount (0.02 x)	
Net cost of machine tool	

Aug.	2					
	3					
	7					
	10					
			Made payment on account to			
			Gear Company			
				−	=	

Chapter 5, SE 5.

Aug.	4				
	4				
	5				
	9				
	9				
Sept.	3				
			Received payment on account from Kwai Corporation		
			−	=	

Chapter 5, SE 6.

Apr.	19				
			Sales for which Visa cards were accepted		
			X	=	

Chapter 5, SE 7.

Aug.	2					
	3					
	7					
	10					
			Made payment on account to Gear Company			
			−	=		

Chapter 5, SE 8.

Purchases:			
Cost of Goods Sold			
Merchandise Inventory,			
Sept. 30, 20xx			
Purchases			
Less Purchases Returns and			
Allowances			
Net Purchases			
Freight In			
Net Cost of Purchases			
Goods Available for Sale			
Less Merchandise Inventory,			
Oct. 31, 20xx			
Cost of Goods Sold			

Chapter 5, SE 9.

Aug.	4					
	5					
	9					
Sept.	3					
			Received payment on account from Kwai Corporation			
				−	=	

Chapter 5, SE 10.

1. The perpetual inventory system

2. The periodic inventory system

Chapter 5, SE 11.

Hassi Company records:

Apr.	15						
	20						
	25						
			Received payment on account from Swallow Company; discount taken				
			−		=		
			x	2%	=		
			−		=		

Swallow Company records:

Apr.	15						
	20						
	25						

Chapter 5, E 1.

1.		4.	
2.		5.	
3.		6.	

Chapter 5, E 2.

1. **Operating report prepared**

Bearclaw Hardware Company Operating Budget For the Six Months Ended June 30, 20x1			
	Budget	**Actual**	**Difference Under (Over) Budget**
Operating Expenses			
Selling Expenses			
General and Administrative Expenses			
Total Operating Expenses			

2.   Operating budget discussed

a.	
b.	
c.	
d.	
e.	
f.	
g.	

Chapter 5, E 4.

List price	
Less 30 percent	
Dealer price	
Shipping cost	
Cost of refrigerator	
Less sales discount (0.02 x **)**	
Net cost of refrigerator	

Chapter 5, E 5.

Tents, Etc. Store Income Statement For the Year Ended December 31, 20xx		
Net Sales		

Chapter 5, E 6.

a.

b.

c.

d.

Purchased merchandise, terms n/30, FOB shipping point

—   =

e.

f.

g.

h.

Paid amount owed on transaction *c*

—   =

Chapter 5, E 7.

June	15				
	15				
	20				
	20				
	25				
			Received payment on account from Whist Company		
			− =		

Boston General Store			
Income Statement			
For the Year Ended December 31, 20x2			

Chapter 5, E 9.

	20x3	20x2	20x1
Gross Sales	(p)	(h)	
Sales Returns and Allowances			(a)
Net Sales	(q)		(b)
Merchandise Inventory, Beginning	(r)	(i)	
Purchases			(c)
Purchases Returns and Allowances		(j)	
Freight In	(s)		
Net Cost of Purchases		(k)	(d)
Goods Available for Sale			
Merchandise Inventory, Ending		(l)	
Cost of Goods Sold	(t)		(e)
Gross Margin		(m)	
Selling Expenses	(u)		(f)
General and Administrative Expenses		(n)	
Total Operating Expenses			(g)
Income Before Income Taxes	(v)	(o)	
Income Taxes			
Net Income	(w)		

a.									
b.									
c.									
d.									
		Purchased merchandise, terms n/30, FOB shipping point							
				−		=			
e.									
f.									
g.									
h.									
		Paid amount owed on transaction *c*							
				−		=			

Chapter 5, E 11.

June	15								
	20								
	25								
			Received payment on account from Whist Company						
				−		=			

Chapter 5, E 12.

20xx					
Dec.	31				
	31				
	31				
	31				

20xx					
Dec.	31				
	31				
	31				
	31				

Chapter 5, E 14.

Mar.	**1**					
	3					
	10					
		Received payment on account				
		from Smith Company; discount				
		taken				
			−		=	
			x	2%	=	
			−		=	
	11					
	31					

Chapter 5, E 15.

July	2				
	6				
	11				
			Made payment on account to Ordner Company; discount taken		
			—	=	
			x 2%	=	
			—	=	
	14				
	31				

Chapter 5, E 16.

1.   Entries prepared by the Whalen Company

	Paid for purchase; discount taken			
	Amount owed			
	Discount (	**x**	**)**	
	Cash paid			

2.   Entries prepared by the Midori Company

	Received payment for merchandise;			
	discount taken			
	Amount due			
	Discount (	**x**	**)**	
	Cash received			

1.   Income statement prepared

Alan's Accessories			
Income Statement			
For the Year Ended August 31, 20x2			

2. | **Income statement discussed**

20xx					
Oct.	7				
	7				
	8				
	9				
	10				
	13				
	14				

20xx					
Oct.	14				
	14				
	17				
	18				
	19				
	19				
	20				
	21				
			Made payment on account to Ruff Company for purchase of Oct. 8 net of return on Oct. 14		
			− =		
	24				
	24				

1. Income statement prepared

Carol's Kitchen Shop Income Statement For the Year Ended March 31, 20x4			

Chapter 5, P 3. (Continued)

2. **Income statement discussed**

Chapter 5, P 4.

20xx					
Oct.	7				
	8				
	9				
	10				
	13				
	14				

Chapter 5, P 4. (Continued)

20xx					
Oct.	14				
	17				
	18				
	19				
	20				
	21				
		Made payment on account to Ruff Company for purchase of Oct. 8 net of return on Oct. 14			
		− =			
	24				

1. Work sheet completed

Metzler Music Store
Work Sheet
For the Year Ended November 30, 20x4

Account Name	Trial Balance		Adjustments		Income Statement		Balance Sheet	
	Debit	Credit	Debit	Credit	Debit	Credit	Debit	Credit
Cash								
Net Income								

2. **Income statement, statement of owner's equity, and balance sheet prepared**

Metzler Music Store			
Income Statement			
For the Year Ended November 30, 20x4			

Metzler Music Store
Statement of Owner's Equity
For the Year Ended November 30, 20x4

Metzler Music Store
Balance Sheet
November 30, 20x4

Assets

Liabilities

Owner's Equity

3. **Closing entries prepared**

20x4					
Nov.	30				
	30				
	30				
	30				

1. Work sheet completed

Le Bere Office Supplies Company
Work Sheet
For the Year Ended September 30, 20x4

Account Name	Trial Balance		Adjustments		Income Statement		Balance Sheet	
	Debit	Credit	Debit	Credit	Debit	Credit	Debit	Credit
Cash								
Net Income								

2. Income statement, statement of owner's equity, and balance sheet prepared

Le Bere Office Supplies Company Income Statement For the Year Ended September 30, 20x4			

Le Bere Office Supplies Company
Statement of Owner's Equity
For the Year Ended September 30, 20x4

Le Bere Office Supplies Company
Balance Sheet
September 30, 20x4

Assets

Liabilities

Owner's Equity

3. | **Closing entries prepared**

20x4					
Sept.	30				
	30				
	30				
	30				

20xx						
Mar.	1					
	3					
	4					
	6					
	7					
	9					
	10					
	10					
			Received payment in full from			
			M. Gaberman for sale of March 1;			
			2% discount allowed			
			0.20	x	=	

20xx						
Mar.	11					
	12					
	13					
			Paid for purchase of March 3 from King Company; 2% discount taken			
			0.02 x	=		
	14					
	16					
	17					
			Received payment from B. Gomez for half of March 7 sale; 2% discount taken			
			x	=		
	18					
			Paid for purchase of March 9 less return for March 14; 1% discount taken (on merchandise only)			
			x	=		
	20					

20xx						
Mar.	21					
	23					
	24					
	25					
	27					
	28					
	29					
	31					

1. Multistep income statement prepared

Hans' Video Store			
Income Statement			
For the Year Ended June 30, 20x3			

2. | **Income statement discussed**

20xx					
July	1				
	1				
	3				
	5				
	6				
	8				
	12				
	15				

20xx						
July	**15**					
	16					
	17					
	17					
	18					
	18					
	24					
			Made payment on account to Angier Company			
			–	=		
	25					
			Received payment on account from Su Long			
			–	=		

1. Income statement prepared

Dan's Sports Equipment			
Income Statement			
For the Year Ended September 30, 20x5			

2. **Income statement discussed**

Chapter 5, P 11.

20xx							
July	1						
	3						
	5						
	6						
	8						
	12						
	15						

20xx					
July	16				
	17				
	18				
	24				
		Made payment on account to Angier Company			
			−	=	
	25				
		Received payment on account from Su Long			
			−	=	

Chapter 5, SD 5.

1. **Cost of goods sold recomputed**

	20x6		20x5	
Beginning Inventory				
Gross Purchases				
Less Purchases Allowances				
Net Purchases				
Freight In				
Net Cost of Purchases				
Goods Available for Sale				
Less Ending Inventory				
Cost of Goods Sold				
20x6 Net Income				
Manager's Salary				
Inventory Loss				
20x5 Net Income				

2.   **Possible reasons for the inventory loss suggested**

Chapter 5, FRA 1.

1.		Wal-Mart		Kmart	
		(millions)	%	(millions)	%
	Net Sales		100.0%		100.0%
	Cost of Goods Sold				
	Gross Margin				
	Operating Expenses				
	Income from Operations				
	Inventory				
	Inventory/Cost of Goods Sold				

2.

3.

Chapter 5, FRA 2.

	Year Ended		
	January 30, 2001	January 31, 2000	February 1, 1999
(in millions)			

Chapter 6, SE 1.

1.
2.
3.
4.
5.

Chapter 6, SE 2.

1.
2.
3.
4.
5.
6.
7.
8.
9.
10.

Balance Sheet
May 31, 20xx

Assets

Liabilities

Owner's Equity

238

Chapter 6, SE 4.

1.	
2.	
3.	
4.	
5.	
6.	
7.	
8.	

Chapter 6, SE 5.

Income Statement For the Year Ended May 31, 20xx		

Income Statement
For the Year Ended May 31, 20xx

Chapter 6, SE 7.

Current Assets	=		+		+		+		=	
Working Capital	=	Current Assets		−	Current Liabilities					
	=			−						

Current Ratio	=	Current Assets / Current Liabilities	=	____	=	

Chapter 6, SE 8.

1.	Profit Margin	=	Net Income / Net Sales	=	____ *	=	
*		−		−		=	
2.	Asset Turnover	=	____	=	____ *	=	times
* (		+		)	÷	=	
3.	Return on Assets	=	____	=	____	=	
4.	Debt to Equity	=	____	=	____	=	
5.	Return on Equity	=	____	=	____ *	=	
* (		+		)	÷	=	

Chapter 6, E 1.

1.
2.
3.
4.
5.

Chapter 6, E 2.

1.	12.	
2.	13.	
3.	14.	
4.	15.	
5.	16.	
6.	17.	
7.	18.	
8.	19.	
9.	20.	
10.	21.	
11.	22.	

Chapter 6, E 3.

1.	9.	
2.	10.	
3.	11.	
4.	12.	
5.	13.	
6.	14.	
7.	15.	
8.	16.	

Assets

Liabilities

Stockholders' Equity

Chapter 6, E 5.

1.		9.	
2.		10.	
3.		11.	
4.		12.	
5.		13.	
6.		14.	
7.		15.	
8.		16.	

244

Chapter 6, E 6.

1. Single-step income statement prepared

Revenues		
Costs and Expenses		
Net Income		

2. Multistep income statement prepared

Sales		
Cost of Goods Sold		
Gross Margin		
Operating Expenses		
Income from Operations		
Other Revenues and Expenses		
Net Income		

Rosala Housewares Company
Income Statement
For the Year Ended June 30, 20xx

Net Sales		

Chapter 6, E 8.

1.   Working capital computed

Current Assets		
Current Liabilities		
Working Capital		

2.   Current ratio computed

Current Ratio	=	$\dfrac{\text{Current Assets}}{\text{Current Liabilities}}$	=		=	

Chapter 6, E 9.

1. Profit Margin = — = = * =

  * = = * =

2. Asset Turnover = — = = (+ *) ÷

  * = =

3. Return on Assets = = times

4. Debt to Equity = = =

5. Return on Equity = (+ *) ÷ =

  * — + = =

1. Liquidity measure computed

a.
Current Assets
Current Liabilities
Working Capital

b. Current Ratio $=$ $=$ $\dfrac{\text{Current Assets}}{\text{Current Liabilities}}$ $=$

2. Profitability measures computed

a. Profit Margin $=$ $=$ $=$

b. Asset Turnover $=$ $=$ $($ $+$ $) \div$

$=$ times

c. Return on Assets $=$ $=$

d. Debt to Equity $=$ $=$

e. Return on Equity $=$ $=$ $($ $+$ $) \div$

$=$

249

1.

2.

3.

4.

5.

1. Detailed income statement prepared

Muramoto Hardware Company
Income Statement
For the Year Ended September 30, 20x2

2. Condensed multistep income statement prepared

Muramoto Hardware Company Income Statement For the Year Ended September 30, 20x2		

3. Condensed single-step income statement prepared

Muramoto Hardware Company Income Statement For the Year Ended September 30, 20x2		

Tasheki Hardware Company
Balance Sheet
September 30, 20x2

Assets

(continued)

Liabilities

Owner's Equity

Chapter 6, P 4.

1. Liquidity measures computed

a. Working Capital

	20x4	20x3
Current assets		
Current liabilities		
Working capital		

b.	Current Ratio	=	Current Assets / Current Liabilities

20x4: ——————— =

20x3: ——————— =

2. Profitability measures computed

a.	Profit Margin	=	Net Income / Net Sales

20x4: ——————— =

20x3: ——————— =

b.	**Asset Turnover**	=	

	20x4:	(_____ + _____) ÷ _____	= _____ times

	20x3:	(_____ + _____) ÷ _____	= _____ times

c.	**Return on Assets**	=	

	20x4:	(_____ + _____) ÷ _____	=

	20x3:	(_____ + _____) ÷ _____	=

d.	**Debt to Equity**	=	

	20x4:	_____	=

	20x3:	_____	=

e.	**Return on Equity**	=	

	20x4:	(_____ + _____) ÷ _____	=

	20x3:	(_____ + _____) ÷ _____	=

1a. Multistep income statement prepared

Blossom Lawn Equipment Center		
Income Statement		
For the Year Ended December 31, 20x4		

1b. Statement of owner's equity prepared

Blossom Lawn Equipment Center		
Statement of Owner's Equity		
For the Year Ended December 31, 20x4		

1c. **Classified balance sheet prepared**

Blossom Lawn Equipment Center
Balance Sheet
December 31, 20x4

Assets

Liabilities

Owner's Equity

2. **Liquidity measures computed**

a.	Current assets		
	Current liabilities		
	Working capital		

| b. | Current Ratio | = | $\dfrac{\text{Current Assets}}{\text{Current Liabilities}}$ | = | | = | |

3. **Profitability measures computed**

a.	Profit Margin	=		=		=	
b.	Asset Turnover	=					
		=	(	+	) ÷		=	times
c.	Return on Assets	=					
		=	(	+	) ÷		=	
d.	Debt to Equity	=		=		=	
e.	Return on Equity	=					
		=	(	+	) ÷		=	

1.

2.

3.

4.

5.

1. Detailed income statement prepared

O'Dell Hardware Company
Income Statement
For the Year Ended March 31, 20x3

2. **Condensed multistep income statement prepared**

O'Dell Hardware Company Income Statement For the Year Ended March 31, 20x3		

3. **Condensed single-step income statement prepared**

O'Dell Hardware Company Income Statement For the Year Ended March 31, 20x3		

Chapter 6, P 8.

1. Liquidity measures computed and discussed

a. Working capital		20x4	20x3
Current assets			
Current liabilities			
Working capital			

b.	Current Ratio	=	Current Assets
			Current Liabilities

20x4: ———— =

20x3: ———— =

2. Profitability measures computed and discussed

a.	Profit Margin	=	

20x4: ———— =

20x3: ———— =

b.	**Asset Turnover**	=							

	20x4:	(		+		) ÷		=		times

	20x3:	(		+		) ÷		=		times

c.	**Return on Assets**	=	

	20x4:	(		+		) ÷		=	

	20x3:	(		+		) ÷		=	

d.	**Debt to Equity**	=	

	20x4:		=	

	20x3:		=	

e.	**Return on Equity**	=	

	20x4:	(		+		) ÷		=	

	20x3:	(		+		) ÷		=	

1. Analysis performed

Analysis of Handy Harvey, Inc.

	Before Loan				After Loan		
Liquidity							
Working Capital	–		=		–		=
Current Ratio	+		=		+		=
Profitability							
Profit Margin	+		=				
Asset Turnover	+	(	) +	=			
Return on Assets	+	(	) +	=			
Debt to Equity	+		=		+		=
Return on Equity	+	(	) +	=			

times

Discussion

Analysis of Sheila's Fashions, Inc.

		Before Loan				After Loan		
Liquidity								
	Working Capital	−		=		−		=
	Current Ratio	+		=		−		=
Profitability								
	Profit Margin	+ (		+	) +				
	Asset Turnover	+ (		+	) +				
	Return on Assets	+		+	) +				
	Debt to Equity	+		=		+		=
	Return on Equity	+ (		+	) +	times			
Discussion								

2. **Loan decision recommendation made**

Memorandum

Date:

To:

From:

Re:

1. Profitability ratios computed (in millions) and discussed

	Albertson's					Safeway				
Net Income										
Net Sales										
Profit Margin										
Net Sales										
Average Total Assets	(		+		) ÷		(		+	) ÷
Asset Turnover					times					times
Net Income										
Average Total Assets (from above)										
Return on Assets										
Total Liabilities										
Total Stockholders' Equity										
Debt to Equity										
Net Income										
Average Stockholders' Equity	(		+		) ÷ + =		(		+	) ÷ + =
Return on Equity										

2.   Return on assets discussed

	Profit Margin	x	Asset Turnover	=	Return on Assets
Albertson's		x	times	=	
Safeway		x	times	=	
Industry*		x	times	=	

* **Industry figures provided in Figures 5 through 7 of the text.**

3.   Debt financing discussed

Chapter 6, FRA 2.

To evaluate profitability, the profit margin and return on assets must be computed as follows:

Profit Margin =			
20x4:		=	
20x3:		=	
Return on Assets =			
20x4:	(	+	) ÷	=
20x3:	(	+	) ÷	=

Asset Turnover =

20x4:	(	+	) ÷	=		times
20x3:	(	+	) ÷	=		times

	Profit Margin	X	Asset Turnover	=	Return on Assets	
20x4:		X		=		
20x3:		X		=		

1. **Liquidity and profitability measures computed** (amounts in millions)

		2000	1999	1999–2000 Industry
	Current Assets			
	Current Liabilities			NA
	Working Capital			
Current Ratio =	Current Assets	=	=	1.9 times
	Current Liabilities			
Profit Margin =		=	=	1.2%
Asset Turnover =		(+) + times	(+) + times	1.1 times
Return on Assets =		(=)	(=)	1.3%
Debt to Equity =		=	=	118.8%
Return on Equity =		(+) + =	(+) + =	2.9%

2. | **Executive Summary memorandum prepared**

Memorandum

Date:

To:

From:

Re:

1. Components of U.K. balance sheet identified and discussed

U.K. Balance Sheet Term	U.S. Balance Sheet Term

2. Ratios computed

British pound amounts are in millions

Current Ratio: Current Assets divided by Creditors: Amounts Due Within One Year

1998:		÷		=	
1999:		÷		=	

Debt to Equity: (Creditors: Amounts Due Within One Year + Long-Term Liabilities*) divided by Capital Employed

1998:	(		+		**) ÷		=	
1999:	(		+		†) ÷		=	

Return on Assets: Net Income divided by (Fixed Assets + Current Assets)

1998:		÷ (		+		) =	
1999:		÷ (		+		) =	

Return on Equity: Net Income divided by Capital Employed

1998:		÷		=	
1999:		÷		=	

* Long-Term Liabilities include Creditors: Amounts Due After One Year + Provisions for Liabilities and Charges

**		+		=
†		+		=

Chapter 6, FRA 5.

1. Consolidated balance sheets

a.

	2000	1999	Increase (Decrease)
Current Assets			
Current Liabilities			
Working Capital			

b.

Current Ratio = _____

2000: _____ = _____ 1999: _____ = _____

c.

d.

Debt to Equity = _____

2000: _____ = _____ 1999: _____ = _____

e.

2. **Consolidated statements of earnings**

a.

b.

c.

d.

e.

Profit Margin = $\dfrac{\text{Net Income (Loss)}}{}$

2000: _____ = _____   1999: _____ = _____

f.

Asset Turnover = _____

2000: (_____ + _____) ÷ _____ = _____ **times**

1999: (_____ + _____) ÷ _____ = _____ **times**

g.

Return on Assets = _____

| 2000: | (| + |) ÷ | = |
| 1999: | (| + |) ÷ | = |

h.

Return on Equity = _____

| 2000: | (| + |) ÷ | = |
| 1999: | (| + |) ÷ | = |

3. **Multistep income statements prepared and discussed**

	2000		1999	
	Amount	Percentage	Amount	Percentage
Net Sales		100.0%		100.0%
Cost of Sales				
Gross Margin				
Operating Expenses				
Selling, Advertising, General and Administrative Expenses				
Depreciation and Amortization and Asset Write-offs				
Total Operating Expenses				
Income from Operations				

Toys "R" Us, Inc.
Consolidated Statements of Earnings
For the Years Ended January 29, 2000, and January 30, 1999
(in thousands)

Note: 1999 operating expenses excludes restructuring charges.

Chapter 7, SE 1.

| 1. | | 3. | |
| 2. | | 4. | |

Chapter 7, SE 2.

1.		4.	
2.		5.	
3.		6.	

Chapter 7, SE 3.

1.		4.	
2.		5.	
3.		6.	

Chapter 7, SE 4.

		Sales Journal			
Date		Account Debited	Invoice Number	Post. Ref.	Amount (Debit/Credit Accounts Receivable/Sales)
20xx					

Chapter 7, SE 5.

Purchases Journal

Date	Account Credited	Date of Invoice	Terms	Post. Ref.	Credit: Accounts Payable	Debits: Purchases	Freight In	Store Supplies	Office Supplies	Other Accounts: Account	Post. Ref.	Amount
20xx												
Oct. 2												
4												
6												
9												

Chapter 7, SE 8.

Cash Receipts Journal

| Date | Account Debited/Credited | Post. Ref. | Debits | | | | Credits | | |
			Cash	Sales Discounts	Other Accounts	Accounts Receivable	Sales	Other Accounts
20xx								
Oct. 8								
9								

Cash Payments Journal

Date		Ck. No.	Payee	Account Credited/Debited	Post. Ref.	Credits			Debits	
						Cash	Purchases Discounts	Other Accounts	Accounts Payable	Other Accounts
20xx										
Oct.	8									
	12									

Chapter 7, E 1.

1.
2.
3.
4.
5.
6.
7.
8.
9.
10.
11.
12.

Chapter 7, E 2.

1.
2.
3.
4.

5.

1.		
2.	May 25:	
	May 26:	
	May 27:	
	May 31:	
3.	a.	
	b.	
	c.	
	d.	

Chapter 7, E 4.

1. Purchases journal set up
2. Transactions entered, and columns footed and crossfooted

Purchases Journal

Date	Account Credited	Date of Invoice	Terms	Post. Ref.	Credit — Accounts Payable	Debits — Purchases	Debits — Freight In	Debits — Store Supplies	Debits — Office Supplies	Other Accounts — Account	Other Accounts — Post. Ref.	Other Accounts — Amount
July 1												
3												
18												
23												
27												
31												

Debit Column Totals

Credit Column Totals

Chapter 7, E 5.

1.

2.

3.

4.

5.

288

Chapter 7, E 6.

1. Ledger accounts opened and amounts posted from the sales journal

General Ledger

Accounts Receivable   Account No. 112

Date	Item	Post. Ref.	Debit	Credit	Balance Debit	Balance Credit

Sales   Account No. 411

Date	Item	Post. Ref.	Debit	Credit	Balance Debit	Balance Credit

Accounts Receivable Subsidiary Ledger

Gina Colantos

Date	Item	Post. Ref.	Debit	Credit	Balance

Ed Kohl

Date	Item	Post. Ref.	Debit	Credit	Balance
June 8					

Sue Lang

Date	Item	Post. Ref.	Debit	Credit	Balance
June 3					
18					

Ye Sang

Date	Item	Post. Ref.	Debit	Credit	Balance
June 12					

2.   Accounts receivable subsidiary ledger proved

Fern Corporation
Schedule of Accounts Receivable
June 30, 20xx

Total Accounts Receivable	

Chapter 7, E 7.

1. Sales account entries identified

Oct.	31	
Oct.	31	
Oct.	31	

2. T. Bearn entries identified

Oct.	8	
Oct.	12	
Oct.	18	

Chapter 7, E 8.

1. D. Yousif's transactions identified

Mar.	31	
Apr.	7	
Apr.	12	
Apr.	17	

2. Dao Company transactions identified

Apr.	18	
Apr.	20	
Apr.	25	

Chapter 7, P 1.

1. **Special-purpose journals and general journal prepared**
5. **Transactions entered in journals**
6. **Journals footed and crossfooted**

		Account Debited	Invoice Number	Terms	Post. Ref.	Debit/Credit Accounts Receivable/Sales
Date						
Sept.	2				✓	
	23					

Sales Journal — Page 1

Purchases Journal

Page 1

Date	Account Credited	Date of Invoice	Terms	Post. Ref.	Debit/Credit Purchases/Accounts Payable
Sept. 22					
26					

Cash Receipts Journal

Page 1

Date	Account Debited/Credited	Post. Ref.	Debits Cash	Debits Sales Discounts	Other Accounts	Credits Accounts Receivable	Credits Sales	Credits Other Accounts
Sept. 4								
12								
15								

Cash Payments Journal

Page 1

Date	Ck. No.	Payee	Account Credited/Debited	Post. Ref.	Credits Cash	Credits Purchases Discounts	Other Accounts	Debits Accounts Payable	Debits Other Accounts
Sept. 5									
9									

General Journal
Page 1

Date		Description	Post. Ref.	Debit	Credit
Sept.	8				
	30				

2. **General ledger accounts opened**
5. **Transactions posted**
6. **End-of-month postings made**

General Ledger

Accounts Receivable
Account No. 112

Date		Item	Post. Ref.	Debit	Credit	Balance Debit	Balance Credit
Aug.	31						
Sept.	8						
	30						
	30						

Accounts Payable
Account No. 211

Date		Item	Post. Ref.	Debit	Credit	Balance Debit	Balance Credit
Aug.	31						
Sept.	30						
	30						
	30						

Chapter 7, P 1. (Continued)

3.	Accounts receivable subsidiary ledger accounts opened
5.	Transactions posted

Accounts Receivable Subsidiary Ledger

S. Adams

Date		Item	Post. Ref.	Debit	Credit	Balance
Aug.	31					
Sept.	15					

M. Alwin

Date		Item	Post. Ref.	Debit	Credit	Balance
Aug.	31					
Sept.	2					
	4					
	8					
	12					

I. Yancy

Date		Item	Post. Ref.	Debit	Credit	Balance
Sept.	23					

4. **Accounts payable subsidiary ledger accounts opened**
5. **Transactions posted**

Accounts Payable Subsidiary Ledger

Halcom, Inc.

Date		Item	Post. Ref.	Debit	Credit	Balance
Aug.	31					
Sept.	5					
	26					

Wolcord Company

Date		Item	Post. Ref.	Debit	Credit	Balance
Aug.	31					
Sept.	9					
	22					
	30					

7. **Schedules of accounts receivable and payable prepared**

Lamb Company Schedule of Accounts Receivable September 30, 20xx	
Total Accounts Receivable	

Lamb Company Schedule of Accounts Payable September 30, 20xx	
Total Accounts Payable	

Chapter 7, P 2.

1. Transactions entered in cash receipts and cash payments journals
2. Journals footed and crossfooted

Cash Receipts Journal

Date	Account Debited/Credited	Post. Ref.	Debits		Credits		
			Cash	Sales Discounts	Other Accounts	Accounts Receivable	Sales	Other Accounts
Mar. 1								
3								
10								
12								
19								
20								
27								

Cash Payments Journal

Date	Ck. No.	Payee	Account Credited/Debited	Post. Ref.	Credits			Debits	
					Cash	Purchases Discounts	Other Accounts	Accounts Payable	Other Accounts
Mar. 2	75								
6	76								
7	77								
8	78								
9	79								
13	80								
21	81								
23	82								
26	83								
28	84								
31	85								

Chapter 7, P 3.

1. Transactions entered in general journal and purchases journal

General Journal					Page 1
Date	Description	Post. Ref.	Debit	Credit	
20xx					
Aug. 31					

2. Purchases journal footed and crossfooted

Purchases Journal
Page 1

Date		Account Credited	Date of Invoice	Terms	Post. Ref.	Credit Accounts Payable	Debits Purchases	Freight In	Store Supplies	Office Supplies	Other Accounts Account	Post. Ref.	Amount
20xx													
Aug.	2												
	5												
	8												
	12												
	14												
	17												
	17												
	20												
	24												
	26												
	30												

3. **General ledger and accounts payable subsidiary ledger accounts opened and amounts posted**

General Ledger

Store Supplies — Account No. 116

Date		Item	Post. Ref.	Debit	Credit	Balance Debit	Balance Credit
20xx							
Aug.	31						

Office Supplies — Account No. 117

Date		Item	Post. Ref.	Debit	Credit	Balance Debit	Balance Credit
20xx							
Aug.	31						

Trucks — Account No. 142

Date		Item	Post. Ref.	Debit	Credit	Balance Debit	Balance Credit
20xx							
Aug.	5						

Office Equipment — Account No. 144

Date		Item	Post. Ref.	Debit	Credit	Balance Debit	Balance Credit
20xx							
Aug.	12						

Accounts Payable — Account No. 211

Date		Item	Post. Ref.	Debit	Credit	Balance Debit	Balance Credit
20xx							
Aug.	31						
	31						

Purchases — Account No. 611

Date		Item	Post. Ref.	Debit	Credit	Balance Debit	Balance Credit
20xx							
Aug.	31						

Purchases Returns and Allowances   Account No. 612

Date	Item	Post. Ref.	Debit	Credit	Balance Debit	Balance Credit
20xx						
Aug. 31						

Freight In   Account No. 613

Date	Item	Post. Ref.	Debit	Credit	Balance Debit	Balance Credit
20xx						
Aug. 31						

Accounts Payable Subsidiary Ledger

Alvarez Company

Date	Item	Post. Ref.	Debit	Credit	Balance
20xx					
Aug. 2					
17					
24					

Dandridge Company

Date	Item	Post. Ref.	Debit	Credit	Balance
20xx					
Aug. 8					
12					
26					

Hollins Company

Date	Item	Post. Ref.	Debit	Credit	Balance
20xx					
Aug. 17					

Meriweather Company

Date	Item	Post. Ref.	Debit	Credit	Balance
20xx					
Aug. 5					

Petrie Company

Date		Item	Post. Ref.	Debit	Credit	Balance
20xx						
Aug.	14					
	20					
	30					
	31					

Chapter 7, P 4.

1. **Special-purpose journals and general journal prepared**
5. **Transactions entered in journals**
6. **Journals footed and crossfooted**

		Sales Journal				Page 1
Date		Account Debited	Invoice Number	Terms	Post. Ref.	Amount (Debit/Credit Accounts Receivable/Sales)
20xx						
July	10					
	11					
	25					
	27					

Purchases Journal

Page 1

Date	Account Credited	Date of Invoice	Terms	Post. Ref.	Credit: Accounts Payable	Debits: Purchases	Debits: Freight In	Debits: Other Accounts Account	Debits: Other Accounts Post. Ref.	Debits: Other Accounts Amount
20xx July 4										
5										
12										
17										
18										
19										

Cash Receipts Journal

Page 1

Date	Account Debited/Credited	Post. Ref.	Debits: Cash	Debits: Sales Discounts	Debits: Other Accounts	Credits: Accounts Receivable	Credits: Sales	Credits: Other Accounts
20xx July 2								
7								
8								
15								
20								
22								
29								

Chapter 7, P 4. (Continued)

Cash Payments Journal

Page 1

Date	Ck. No.	Payee	Account Credited/Debited	Post. Ref.	Cash	Credits Purchases Discounts	Credits Other Accounts	Debits Accounts Payable	Debits Other Accounts
20xx									
July 3									
6									
13									
24									
26									
28									
31									

305

		General Journal			Page 1
Date		Description	Post. Ref.	Debit	Credit
20xx					
July	14				
	21				

Chapter 7, P 4. (Continued)

2. **General ledger accounts opened**
5. **Transactions posted**
6. **End-of-month postings made**

General Ledger

Cash Account No. 111

Date		Item	Post. Ref.	Debit	Credit	Balance Debit	Balance Credit
20xx							
July	31						
	31						

Accounts Receivable Account No. 112

Date		Item	Post. Ref.	Debit	Credit	Balance Debit	Balance Credit
20xx							
July	14						
	31						
	31						

Store Equipment Account No. 141

Date		Item	Post. Ref.	Debit	Credit	Balance Debit	Balance Credit
20xx							
July	6						

Accounts Payable Account No. 211

Date		Item	Post. Ref.	Debit	Credit	Balance Debit	Balance Credit
20xx							
July	21						
	31						
	31						

Notes Payable Account No. 212

Date		Item	Post. Ref.	Debit	Credit	Balance Debit	Balance Credit
20xx							
July	7						

Carlos Lezcano, Capital — Account No. 311

Date	Item	Post. Ref.	Debit	Credit	Balance Debit	Balance Credit
20xx						
July 2						

Sales — Account No. 411

Date	Item	Post. Ref.	Debit	Credit	Balance Debit	Balance Credit
20xx						
July 31						
31						

Sales Discounts — Account No. 412

Date	Item	Post. Ref.	Debit	Credit	Balance Debit	Balance Credit
20xx						
July 31						

Sales Returns and Allowances — Account No. 413

Date	Item	Post. Ref.	Debit	Credit	Balance Debit	Balance Credit
20xx						
July 14						

Purchases — Account No. 511

Date	Item	Post. Ref.	Debit	Credit	Balance Debit	Balance Credit
20xx						
July 31						

Purchases Discounts — Account No. 512

Date	Item	Post. Ref.	Debit	Credit	Balance Debit	Balance Credit
20xx						
July 31						

Chapter 7, P 4. (Continued)

Purchases Returns and Allowances — Account No. 513

Date		Item	Post. Ref.	Debit	Credit	Balance Debit	Balance Credit
20xx							
July	21						

Freight In — Account No. 514

Date		Item	Post. Ref.	Debit	Credit	Balance Debit	Balance Credit
20xx							
July	31						

Sales Salaries Expense — Account No. 611

Date		Item	Post. Ref.	Debit	Credit	Balance Debit	Balance Credit
20xx							
July	31						

Advertising Expense — Account No. 612

Date		Item	Post. Ref.	Debit	Credit	Balance Debit	Balance Credit
20xx							
July	12						

Rent Expense — Account No. 613

Date		Item	Post. Ref.	Debit	Credit	Balance Debit	Balance Credit
20xx							
July	3						

Chapter 7, P 4. (Continued)

3.	Accounts receivable subsidiary ledger accounts opened
5.	Transactions posted

Accounts Receivable Subsidiary Ledger

Al Kaiser

Date		Item	Post. Ref.	Debit	Credit	Balance
20xx						
July	27					

Midlands School

Date		Item	Post. Ref.	Debit	Credit	Balance
20xx						
July	10					
	20					
	25					

Charlotte Soo

Date		Item	Post. Ref.	Debit	Credit	Balance
20xx						
July	11					
	14					

Chapter 7, P 4. (Continued)

4. Accounts payable subsidiary ledger accounts opened

5. Transactions posted

Accounts Payable Subsidiary Ledger

Garnett Company

Date		Item	Post. Ref.	Debit	Credit	Balance
20xx						
July	4					
	13					
	17					
	21					
	26					

Journal-Citizen

Date		Item	Post. Ref.	Debit	Credit	Balance
20xx						
July	12					
	28					

Law Company

Date		Item	Post. Ref.	Debit	Credit	Balance
20xx						
July	19					

Wiggins Company

Date		Item	Post. Ref.	Debit	Credit	Balance
20xx						
July	5					
	18					
	24					

7.   Trial balance and schedules of accounts receivable and payable prepared

Lezcano's Men's Wear		
Trial Balance		
July 31, 20xx		

Lezcano's Men's Wear	
Schedule of Accounts Receivable	
July 31, 20xx	
Total Accounts Receivable	

Lezcano's Men's Wear	
Schedule of Accounts Payable	
July 31, 20xx	

Chapter 7, P 5.

1. Special-purpose journals and general journal prepared
5. Transactions entered in journals
6. Journals footed and crossfooted

		Sales Journal				Page 1
Date		Account Debited	Invoice Number	Post. Ref.	Amount (Debit/Credit Accounts Receivable/Sales)	
20xx						
May	8					
	10					
	16					
	26					

Purchases Journal

Page 1

Date		Account Credited	Date of Invoice	Terms	Post. Ref.	Credit Accounts Payable	Purchases	Freight In	Other Accounts Debits		
									Account	Post. Ref.	Amount
20xx											
May	1										
	3										
	12										
	20										
	21										
	23										

Cash Receipts Journal

Page 1

Date		Account Debited/Credited	Post. Ref.	Debits			Credits		
				Cash	Sales Discounts	Other Accounts	Accounts Receivable	Sales	Other Accounts
20xx									
May	15								
	17								
	19								
	30								
	31								

Chapter 7, P 5. (Continued)

Cash Payments Journal

Page 1

Date	Ck. No.	Payee	Account Credited/Debited	Post. Ref.	Cash	Credits: Purchases Discounts	Credits: Other Accounts	Debits: Accounts Payable	Debits: Other Accounts
20xx									
May 2	230								
5	231								
7	232								
9	233								
11	234								
22	235								
24	236								
28	237								
29	238								
31	239								

		General Journal	Post. Ref.	Debit	Credit
Date		**Description**			
20xx					
May	6				
	14				
	27				

Chapter 7, P 5. (Continued)

2.　**General ledger accounts opened**
5.　**Transactions posted**
6.　**End-of-month postings made**

General Ledger

Cash   Account No. 111

Date		Item	Post. Ref.	Debit	Credit	Balance Debit	Balance Credit
20xx							
May	31						
	31						

Accounts Receivable   Account No. 112

Date		Item	Post. Ref.	Debit	Credit	Balance Debit	Balance Credit
20xx							
May	14						
	31						
	31						

Office Equipment   Account No. 141

Date		Item	Post. Ref.	Debit	Credit	Balance Debit	Balance Credit
20xx							
May	28						

Accounts Payable   Account No. 211

Date		Item	Post. Ref.	Debit	Credit	Balance Debit	Balance Credit
20xx							
May	6						
	27						
	31						
	31						

Sales — Account No. 411

Date		Item	Post. Ref.	Debit	Credit	Balance Debit	Balance Credit
20xx							
May	31						
	31						

Sales Discounts — Account No. 412

Date		Item	Post. Ref.	Debit	Credit	Balance Debit	Balance Credit
20xx							
May	31						

Sales Returns and Allowances — Account No. 413

Date		Item	Post. Ref.	Debit	Credit	Balance Debit	Balance Credit
20xx							
May	14						

Purchases — Account No. 511

Date		Item	Post. Ref.	Debit	Credit	Balance Debit	Balance Credit
20xx							
May	31						

Purchases Discounts — Account No. 512

Date		Item	Post. Ref.	Debit	Credit	Balance Debit	Balance Credit
20xx							
May	31						

Purchases Returns and Allowances — Account No. 513

Date		Item	Post. Ref.	Debit	Credit	Balance Debit	Balance Credit
20xx							
May	6						
	27						

Freight In — Account No. 514

Date		Item	Post. Ref.	Debit	Credit	Balance Debit	Balance Credit
20xx							
May	7						
	31						

Sales Salaries Expense — Account No. 521

Date		Item	Post. Ref.	Debit	Credit	Balance Debit	Balance Credit
20xx							
May	31						

Advertising Expense — Account No. 522

Date		Item	Post. Ref.	Debit	Credit	Balance Debit	Balance Credit
20xx							
May	12						

Rent Expense — Account No. 531

Date		Item	Post. Ref.	Debit	Credit	Balance Debit	Balance Credit
20xx							
May	2						

Repairs Expense — Account No. 532

Date		Item	Post. Ref.	Debit	Credit	Balance Debit	Balance Credit
20xx							
May	5						

Chapter 7, P 5. (Continued)

| 3. | Accounts receivable subsidiary ledger accounts opened |
| 5. | Transactions posted |

Accounts Receivable Subsidiary Ledger

R. Bell

Date		Item	Post. Ref.	Debit	Credit	Balance
20xx						
May	10					
	14					
	19					

C. Share

Date		Item	Post. Ref.	Debit	Credit	Balance
20xx						
May	8					
	17					
	26					

L. Stokes

Date		Item	Post. Ref.	Debit	Credit	Balance
20xx						
May	16					
	30					

Chapter 7, P 5. (Continued)

4.	Accounts payable subsidiary ledger accounts opened
5.	Transactions posted

Accounts Payable Subsidiary Ledger

Costello Company

Date	Item	Post. Ref.	Debit	Credit	Balance
20xx					
May 1					
9					
20					
29					

Noh Company

Date	Item	Post. Ref.	Debit	Credit	Balance
20xx					
May 21					
24					

Vranes Manufacturing

Date	Item	Post. Ref.	Debit	Credit	Balance
20xx					
May 3					
6					
11					
23					
27					

WXYR

Date	Item	Post. Ref.	Debit	Credit	Balance
20xx					
May 12					
22					

7. **Trial balance and schedules of accounts receivable and payable prepared**

Chung Refrigerating Company		
Trial Balance		
May 31, 20xx		

Chung Refrigerating Company	
Schedule of Accounts Receivable	
May 31, 20xx	

Chung Refrigerating Company	
Schedule of Accounts Payable	
May 31, 20xx	
Total Accounts Payable	

Chapter 7, P 6.

1. **Special-purpose journals and general journal prepared**
5. **Transactions entered in journals**
6. **Journals footed and crossfooted**

		Account Debited	Invoice Number	Terms	Post. Ref.	Debit/Credit Accounts Receivable/Sales	
Sales Journal							Page 1
Date		Account Debited	Invoice Number	Terms	Post. Ref.	Debit/Credit Accounts Receivable/Sales	
July	2						
	23						

Purchases Journal

Page 1

Date	Account Credited	Date of Invoice	Terms	Post. Ref.	Purchases/Accounts Payable Debit/Credit
July 22					
26					

Cash Receipts Journal

Page 1

Date	Account Debited/Credited	Post. Ref.	Debits			Credits		
			Cash	Sales Discounts	Other Accounts	Accounts Receivable	Sales	Other Accounts
July 4								
12								
15								

Cash Payments Journal

Page 1

Date	Ck. No.	Payee	Account Credited/Debited	Post. Ref.	Credits			Debits	
					Cash	Purchases Discounts	Other Accounts	Accounts Payable	Other Accounts
July 5	201								
9	202								

General Journal
Page 1

Date	Description	Post. Ref.	Debit	Credit
July 8				
31				

2. **General ledger accounts opened**
5. **Transactions posted**
6. **End-of-month postings made**

General Ledger

Accounts Receivable
Account No. 112

Date	Item	Post. Ref.	Debit	Credit	Balance Debit	Balance Credit
June 30						
July 8						
31						
31						

Accounts Payable
Account No. 211

Date	Item	Post. Ref.	Debit	Credit	Balance Debit	Balance Credit
June 30						
July 31						
31						
31						

Chapter 7, P 6. (Continued)

3.   Accounts receivable subsidiary ledger accounts opened
5.   Transactions posted

Accounts Receivable Subsidiary Ledger

R. Costa

Date		Item	Post. Ref.	Debit	Credit	Balance
June	30					
July	15					

Y. Paik

Date		Item	Post. Ref.	Debit	Credit	Balance
June	30					
July	4					
	23					

L. Stone

Date		Item	Post. Ref.	Debit	Credit	Balance
July	2					
	8					
	12					

| 4. | Accounts payable subsidiary ledger accounts opened |
| 5. | Transactions posted |

Accounts Payable Subsidiary Ledger

Donlevy Company

Date		Item	Post. Ref.	Debit	Credit	Balance
June	30					
July	5					
	22					

Mintol Company

Date		Item	Post. Ref.	Debit	Credit	Balance
June	30					
July	9					
	26					
	31					

| 7. | Schedules of accounts receivable and payable prepared |

Dune Company
Schedule of Accounts Receivable
July 31, 20xx

Total Accounts Receivable	

Dune Company
Schedule of Accounts Payable
July 31, 20xx

Total Accounts Payable	

1. Transactions entered
2. Journals footed and crossfooted

Cash Receipts Journal

Page 1

Date	Account Debited/Credited	Post. Ref.	Debits				Credits		
			Cash	Sales Discounts	Other Accounts		Accounts Receivable	Sales	Other Accounts
Apr. 4									
5									
9									
14									
17									
18									
19									
24									

Cash Payments Journal

Page 1

Date		Ck. No.	Payee	Account Credited/Debited	Post. Ref.	Credits			Debits	
						Cash	Purchases Discounts	Other Accounts	Accounts Payable	Other Accounts
Apr.	1	782								
	3	783								
	8	784								
	11	785								
	15	786								
	16	787								
	20	788								
	21	789								
	25	790								
	26	791								
	27	792								
	30	793								

1. Special-purpose journals and general journal prepared
5. Transactions entered in journals
6. Journals footed and crossfooted

		Sales Journal				Page 1
Date		Account Debited	Invoice Number	Terms	Post. Ref.	Amount (Debit/Credit Accounts Receivable/Sales)
20xx						
Sept.	9					
	17					
	20					
	24					

Purchases Journal

Page 1

Date	Account Credited	Date of Invoice	Terms	Post. Ref.	Credit — Accounts Payable	Debits — Purchases	Debits — Freight In	Other Accounts — Account	Post. Ref.	Amount
20xx										
Sept. 3										
4										
5										
22										
25										

Cash Receipts Journal

Page 1

Date		Account Debited/Credited	Post. Ref.	Debits			Credits		
				Cash	Sales Discounts	Other Accounts	Accounts Receivable	Sales	Other Accounts
20xx									
Sept.	1								
	13								
	16								
	19								
	27								
	30								

Cash Payments Journal

Page 1

Date		Ck. No.	Payee	Account Credited/Debited	Post. Ref.	Credits			Debits	
						Cash	Purchases Discounts	Other Accounts	Accounts Payable	Other Accounts
Sept.	2	C001								
	6	C002								
	8	C003								
	11	C004								
	12	C005								
	15	C006								
	26	C007								
	29	C008								

		General Journal			Page 1
Date		**Description**	**Post. Ref.**	**Debit**	**Credit**
20xx					
Sept.	**10**				
	18				
	23				

2. **General ledger accounts opened**
5. **Transactions posted**
6. **End-of-month postings made**

General Ledger

Cash   Account No. 111

			Post.			Balance	
Date		**Item**	**Ref.**	**Debit**	**Credit**	**Debit**	**Credit**
20xx							
Sept.	**30**						
	30						

Accounts Receivable   Account No. 112

			Post.			Balance	
Date		**Item**	**Ref.**	**Debit**	**Credit**	**Debit**	**Credit**
20xx							
Sept.	**18**						
	30						
	30						

Store Equipment   Account No. 141

Date		Item	Post. Ref.	Debit	Credit	Balance Debit	Balance Credit
20xx							
Sept.	8						

Accounts Payable   Account No. 211

Date		Item	Post. Ref.	Debit	Credit	Balance Debit	Balance Credit
20xx							
Sept.	10						
	23						
	30						
	30						

Notes Payable   Account No. 212

Date		Item	Post. Ref.	Debit	Credit	Balance Debit	Balance Credit
20xx							
Sept.	16						

Cynthia Scott, Capital   Account No. 311

Date		Item	Post. Ref.	Debit	Credit	Balance Debit	Balance Credit
20xx							
Sept.	1						

Sales   Account No. 411

Date		Item	Post. Ref.	Debit	Credit	Balance Debit	Balance Credit
20xx							
Sept.	30						
	30						

Sales Discounts Account No. 412

Date	Item	Post. Ref.	Debit	Credit	Balance Debit	Balance Credit
20xx						
Sept. 30						

Sales Returns and Allowances Account No. 413

Date	Item	Post. Ref.	Debit	Credit	Balance Debit	Balance Credit
20xx						
Sept. 18						

Purchases Account No. 511

Date	Item	Post. Ref.	Debit	Credit	Balance Debit	Balance Credit
20xx						
Sept. 30						

Purchases Discounts Account No. 512

Date	Item	Post. Ref.	Debit	Credit	Balance Debit	Balance Credit
20xx						
Sept. 30						

Purchases Returns and Allowances Account No. 513

Date	Item	Post. Ref.	Debit	Credit	Balance Debit	Balance Credit
20xx						
Sept. 10						
23						

Freight In Account No. 514

Date	Item	Post. Ref.	Debit	Credit	Balance Debit	Balance Credit
20xx						
Sept. 6						
26						
30						

Sales Salaries Expense | Account No. 611

Date		Item	Post. Ref.	Debit	Credit	Balance Debit	Balance Credit
20xx							
Sept.	29						

Advertising Expense | Account No. 612

Date		Item	Post. Ref.	Debit	Credit	Balance Debit	Balance Credit
20xx							
Sept.	11						

Rent Expense | Account No. 613

Date		Item	Post. Ref.	Debit	Credit	Balance Debit	Balance Credit
20xx							
Sept.	2						

Chapter 7, P 8. (Continued)

3. Accounts receivable subsidiary ledger accounts opened
5. Transactions posted

Accounts Receivable Subsidiary Ledger

Joyce Monsoya

Date		Item	Post. Ref.	Debit	Credit	Balance
20xx						
Sept.	20					

Joe Prokop

Date		Item	Post. Ref.	Debit	Credit	Balance
20xx						
Sept.	17					

Spectrum Center

Date		Item	Post. Ref.	Debit	Credit	Balance
20xx						
Sept.	9					
	18					
	19					
	24					

Chapter 7, P 8. (Continued)

4. Accounts payable subsidiary ledger accounts opened

5. Transactions posted

Accounts Payable Subsidiary Ledger

All Points Shippers

Date		Item	Post. Ref.	Debit	Credit	Balance
20xx						
Sept.	4					
	26					

Choice Books

Date		Item	Post. Ref.	Debit	Credit	Balance
20xx						
Sept.	5					
	15					

Gray Books, Inc.

Date		Item	Post. Ref.	Debit	Credit	Balance
20xx						
Sept.	3					
	10					
	12					
	23					
	25					

Temple Publishing Company

Date		Item	Post. Ref.	Debit	Credit	Balance
20xx						
Sept.	22					

7. | **Trial balance and schedules of accounts receivable and payable prepared**

Scott Bookstore		
Trial Balance		
September 30, 20xx		

Scott Bookstore	
Schedule of Accounts Receivable	
September 30, 20xx	
Total Accounts Receivable	

Scott Bookstore	
Schedule of Accounts Payable	
September 30, 20xx	
Total Accounts Payable	

Chapter 8, SE 1.

Chapter 8, SE 2.

1.		4.		
2.		5.		
3.				

Chapter 8, SE 3.

1.		5.		
2.		6.		
3.		7.		
4.				

Chapter 8, SE 4.

1.		3.		
2.		4.		

Chapter 8, SE 5.

	Where Prepared		Where Sent	
1.				
2.				
3.				
4.				
5.				

Chapter 8, SE 6.

1.		3.		
2.		4.		

Chapter 8, SE 7.

Balance per bank, June 30	
Add deposits in transit	
Less outstanding checks	
Adjusted bank balance, June 30	
Balance per books, June 30	
Add interest on average balance	
Adjusted book balance, June 30	

Chapter 8, SE 8.

20xx				
May	31			

Chapter 8, SE 9.

1.		3.	
2.		4.	

Chapter 8, SE 10.

The proper order of the actions is:

Chapter 8, E 1.

1.

2.

3.

4.

Chapter 8, E 2.

1.
2.
3.
4.

Chapter 8, E 3.

1.
2.
3.
4.
5.

Chapter 8, E 4.

Chapter 8, E 5.

Chapter 8, E 6.

Balance per bank, August 31	
Add deposits in transit	
Less outstanding checks	
Adjusted bank balance, August 31	
Balance per books, August 31	
Less bank service charge	
Adjusted book balance, August 31	

Chapter 8, E 7.

a.

b.

c.

d.

Chapter 8, E 8.

Chapter 8, E 9.

July	31				

Chapter 8, E 10.

20xx						
June	1					
	30					
July	31					

1. **Bank reconciliation prepared**

Miguel Beirios Company Bank Reconciliation March 31, 20xx		
Balance per bank, March 31, 20xx		
Add:		
Adjusted bank balance, March 31, 20xx		
Balance per books, March 31, 20xx		
Add:		
Less:		
Adjusted book balance, March 31, 20xx		

2. Journal entries prepared

20xx					
Mar.	31				
	31				
	31				
			To correct an incorrect entry for purchase of merchandise		
			−	=	
	31				
	31				

3. Correct cash balance identified

The adjusted balance of _____ should appear on the balance sheet.

1. | Bank reconciliation prepared

Janesville Company		
Bank Reconciliation		
February 28, 20xx		
Balance per bank, February 28, 20xx		
Add deposit in transit		
Less outstanding checks	No. 2073	
	2078	
	2083	
Adjusted bank balance, February 28, 20xx		
Balance per books, February 28, 20xx		
Add:		
Less:		
Adjusted book balance, February 28, 20xx		

2.   Journal entries prepared

20xx					
Feb.	28				
	28				
	28				
	28				
			NSF check returned by bank plus		
			NSF check fee		
			+	=	
	28				

3.   Cash balance identified

The adjusted balance of		should appear on the balance sheet.

20xx						
Oct.	1					
	31					
Nov.	30					

Authorization

Recording transactions

Documents and records

Physical controls

Periodic independent verification

Separation of duties

Sound personnel procedures

1. Voucher register, check register, and journal entries prepared

Voucher Register

Page 18

Date	Voucher No.	Payee	Payment Date	Payment Check No.	Credit Vouchers Payable	Purchases	Debits Freight In	Store Supplies	Office Supplies
20xx									
Jan. 2	7901								
3	7902								
5	7903								
6	7904								
9	7905								
16	7906								
16	7907								
22	7908								
23	7909								
26	7910								
27	7911								
30	7912								
31	7913								

(continued)

Voucher Register (Continued)

Date	Voucher No.	Payee	Debits					Other Accounts	
			Sales Salaries Expense	Office Salaries Expense	Maintenance Expense, Selling	Maintenance Expense, Office	Utilities Expense	Name	Amount
20xx									
Jan. 2	7901								
3	7902								
5	7903								
6	7904								
9	7905								
16	7906								
16	7907								
22	7908								
23	7909								
26	7910								
27	7911								
30	7912								
31	7913								

| | | | | Debit | Credits | |
| | Check | | Voucher | Vouchers | Purchases | |
Date	No.	Payee	No.	Payable	Discounts	Cash
20xx						
Jan.	5501					
	5502					
	5503					
	5504					
	5505					
	5506					
	5507					
	5508					
	5509					

Check Register — Page 28

| | | Post. | | |
Date	Description	Ref.	Debit	Credit
20xx				
Jan.				

General Journal — Page 25

Chapter 8, P 5. (Continued)

2. Vouchers Payable account prepared

Vouchers Payable | Account No. 211

Date		Item	Post. Ref.	Debit	Credit	Balance Debit	Balance Credit
20xx							
Jan.	18						
	31						
	31						

3. Schedule of unpaid vouchers prepared

M and S Company
Schedule of Unpaid Vouchers
January 31, 20xx

Payee	Voucher No.	Amount
Total Unpaid Vouchers		

Authorization

Recording transactions

Documents and records

Physical controls

Periodic independent verification

Separation of duties

Sound personnel procedures

Chapter 8, P 7.

1. Bank reconciliation prepared

Sagan Company
Bank Reconciliation
June 30, 20xx

Balance per bank, June 30, 20xx		
Add:		
Less:		
Adjusted bank balance, June 30, 20xx		
Balance per books, June 30, 20xx		
Add:		
Less:		
Adjusted book balance, June 30, 20xx		

2. Journal entries prepared

20xx							
June	30						
	30						
	30						
	30						
	30						
		NSF check of Louise Bryant returned by bank plus NSF check fee					
			+		= $ —		

3. Cash balance identified

The adjusted balance of _____ should appear on the balance sheet.

Chapter 8, P 8.

20xx						
Nov.	1					
	30					
Dec.	31					

Chapter 9, SE 1.

1.
2.
3.
4.

Chapter 9, SE 2.

Quick Ratio =

= ___ + ___ + ___

= ___ = ___

Receivable Turnover =

= (___ + ___) + ___

= ___ = ___ times

Average Days' Sales Uncollected =

= ___ days = ___ days

Chapter 9, SE 3.

Chapter 9, SE 4.

May	31							
June	30							
			Accrual of interest on U.S. Treasury bills					
				X		=		
Sept.	28							

Chapter 9, SE 5.

20x1 Dec.	31							
20x2 Mar.	23							

Chapter 9, SE 6.

Oct.	31							
			To record estimated uncollectible accounts expense					
				X		=		

Chapter 9, SE 7.

(a)

June	30				
			To record estimated uncollectible accounts expense		
			−	=	

(b)

June	30				
			To record estimated uncollectible accounts expense		
			+	=	

Chapter 9, SE 8.

May	31				
Aug.	13				
	13				

Chapter 9, SE 9.

Aug.	**25**							
Sept.	**30**							
			To record accrual of 36 days' interest on note					
				x	0.09	x	=	
Nov.	**23**							
			Received payment for note and interest					
			(	x	x	) −		
			=					

Chapter 9, E 1.

1.	
2.	
3.	
4.	
5.	
6.	
7.	
8.	

Chapter 9, E 2.

Quick Ratio	=						
	=		+		+		+
	=		=				
Receivable Turnover	=						
	=						
	(		+		) ÷		
	=		=	times			
Average Days' Sales Uncollected	=						
	=	days	=	days*			

*Rounded.

Chapter 9, E 3.

Chapter 9, E 4.

20x1					
Nov.	1				
Dec.	31				
		Accrual of interest on U.S. Treasury bills			
		x 60/180 =			
20x2					
Apr.	30				

Chapter 9, E 5.

Jan.	6				
		Purchase of Quaker Oats shares as trading securities			
			x	=	
Feb.	15				
		Purchase of EG&G shares as trading securities			
			x	=	
June	30				
		Recognition of unrealized gain on trading portfolio			

Security		Cost	Market Value	
Quaker Oats	(shares)			
EG&G	(shares)			
Totals				

Aug.	20				

Chapter 9, E 6.

		To record estimated uncollectible accounts expense		
		0.007 x		

The balance of allowance for uncollectible accounts after this adjustment is

Chapter 9, E 7.

a.

b.

Chapter 9, E 8.

T accounts prepared to determine ending balances:

Accounts Receivable

Allowance for Uncollectible Accounts

a. Percentage of net sales method applied

Adjusting entry:

		To record estimated uncollectible accounts expense				
			x	0.012	=	

Balance sheet presentation:

Allowance for Uncollectible Accounts			

b. **Aging of accounts receivable method applied**

Adjusting entry:

Balance sheet presentation:

Allowance for Uncollectible Accounts			

Chapter 9, E 9.

a.

		To record estimated uncollectible				
		accounts expense for the year				
		x	0.015	=		

The balance of Allowance for Uncollectible Accounts after this adjustment is _____ (_____ – _____).

b.

		To record estimated uncollectible				
		accounts expense for the year				
		+		=		

The balance of Allowance for Uncollectible Accounts after this adjustment is _____ (_____ – _____).

Chapter 9, E 10.

Journal entries for uncollectible accounts prepared

a.   Percentage of net sales method:

July	31							
			To record estimated uncollectible					
			accounts expense					
				x	0.014	=		

The resulting balance of Allowance for Uncollectible Accounts is

(–   ) .

If the beginning balance of Allowance for Uncollectible Accounts had been a credit, the entry would have been the same, but the resulting balance would have been   (+   ) .

b.   Accounts receivable aging method:

July	31							
			To record estimated uncollectible					
			accounts expense. The debit balance					
			in the allowance account must be					
			added to the estimated uncollectible					
			accounts					
				+		=		

The resulting balance of Allowance for Uncollectible Accounts is

(–   ) .

If the beginning balance of Allowance for Uncollectible Accounts had been a credit, the entry would have been   (–   ) , but the ending balance would have been the same, or   (

+   ) .

Chapter 9, E 11.

20x4						
July	12					
Oct.	18					
20x5						
May	8					
June	22					
	22					

Chapter 9, E 12.

a.		x	/	100	x		/	360	=	
b.		x	/		x		/		=	
c.		x	/		x		/		=	
d.		x	/		x		/		=	
e.		x	/		x		/		=	

Chapter 9, E 13.

Jan.	16									
Feb.	15									
May	16									
			Katz Corporation dishonored note							
				x	/ 100	x	/ 360			
		=								
June	15									
			Received payment in full from Katz Corporation							
				x	/	x	/			
		=								

Chapter 9, E 14.

Dec.	1										
	31										
		To record accrual of 30 days' interest									
		on note									
			x		/	100	x		/	360	
		=									
Mar.	1										
		Received payment for note and									
		interest									
			x		/		x		/		
		=									

Jan.	5										
Mar.	6										
		S. Lavelle paid note plus interest									
			x		/	100	x		/	360	
		=									
	9										
May	8										
		Note from R. Tamayo dishonored									
			x		/		x		/		
		=									
June	7										
		Received from R. Tamayo payment in full plus interest									
			x		/		x		/		
		=									

1. Entries in journal form prepared

20x1					
Jan.	16				
Apr.	15				
		Invested in the following trading securities:			
		10,000 shares of Rani Tools			
		5,000 shares of Soder Gas			
		Total investment			
May	16				
June	2				
		Received cash dividends as follows:			
		Rani Tools			
		Soder Gas			
		Total dividends			
	30				
		Recognition of unrealized loss on trading portfolio:			
		Security		Cost	Market Value
		Rani Tools (10,000 shares)			
		Soder Gas (5,000 shares)			
		Totals			

20x1					
Nov.	14				
20x2					
Feb.	15				
Apr.	1				
June	1				
	30				
		Accrual of interest on U.S. Treasury bills			
		x / 120 =			
	30				
		Recognition of unrealized gain on trading portfolio:			

Security	Cost	Market Value	
Soder Gas (5,000 shares)			
MKD Communications (9,000 shares)			
Totals			
Credit balance of Allowance to Adjust			
Short-Term Investments from 20x1			
Excess of market value over cost in			
20x2			
Total adjustment			

2.	Balance sheet presentation shown		

Short-Term Investments (at cost)*		
Plus Allowance to Adjust Short-Term Investments to Market		
Short-Term Investments (at market)		
or		
Short-Term Investments (at market, cost* is $798,875)		

* Note that Short-Term Investments (at cost) includes the cost of U.S. Treasury bills adjusted for the effects of interest, as follows:

Security	Gost	
U.S. Treasury bills		
Soder Gas (5,000 shares)		
MKD Communications (9,000 shares)		
Total		

1. T accounts prepared and data entered

Accounts Receivable				Allowance for Uncollectible Accounts		
Bal.						

2. Uncollectible Accounts Expense and ending balance of Allowance for Uncollectible Accounts determined

a. Percentage of net sales method:

Uncollectible Accounts Expense	=	1.6 percent	×	Net Credit Sales	
	=	0.016	× (	–	–)

Allowance for Uncollectible Accounts	=		+	–

Accounts Receivable, Net	=			–

b. Accounts receivable aging method:

Uncollectible Accounts Expense	=			–

Allowance for Uncollectible Accounts	=			–

Accounts Receivable, Net	=			–

3. **Receivable turnover and average days' sales uncollected calculated**

Receivable Turnover $=$			$-$				
	(	* $+$		**) $\div$			
$=$		$=$		times			
Average Days' Sales Uncollected $=$	days		$=$		days[†]		
*	$-$		$=$				
**	$-$		$=$				
[†] **Rounded.**							

4. **Difference in methods and rationales discussed**

1. **Aging analysis completed**

			1–30 Days Past Due	31–60 Days Past Due	61–90 Days Past Due	Over 90 Days Past Due

Thant Company
Aging Analysis of Accounts Receivable
December 31, 20xx

Customer Account	Total	Not Yet Due	1–30 Days Past Due	31–60 Days Past Due	61–90 Days Past Due	Over 90 Days Past Due
Balance Forward						

2. **End-of-year balances computed**

Accounts Receivable		
Allowance for Uncollectible Accounts		

Chapter 9, P 3. (Continued)

3. Analysis of estimated uncollectible accounts prepared

Thant Company
Estimated Uncollectible Accounts
December 31, 20xx

	Amount	Percentage Considered Uncollectible	Allowance for Uncollectible Accounts

4. Entry in journal form for uncollectible accounts expense prepared

Dec.	31			
		To record estimated uncollectible accounts expense:		
		Desired balance		
		Debit balance in allowance account		
		Amount of adjustment		

Jan.	**10**				
	20				
Apr.	**20**				
			Received payment for note and interest from Anton Company		
			x / 100 x / 360		
			=		
May	**5**				
	15				
July	**14**				
			Yu Company dishonored note		
			x / x /		
			=		

Aug.	2											
	5											
Nov.	3											
			Vila Company dishonored note									
				x		/	100	x		/	360	
			=									
	9											
			Collection on account from Vila Company, including 15 percent interest for 6 days									
				x		/		x		/		
			=									

1. Entries in journal form prepared

20x1					
Feb.	1				
Mar.	30				
		Invested in the following trading securities:			
		20,000 shares of Files Company			
		12,000 shares of Sun's Fruit, Inc.			
		Total investment			
June	1				
	10				
		Received cash dividends as follows:			
		Files Company			
		Sun's Fruit, Inc.			
		Total dividends			
	30				
		Recognition of unrealized loss on trading portfolio:			
		Security	Cost	Market Value	
		Files Company (20,000 shares)			
		Sun's Fruit, Inc. (12,000 shares)			
		Totals			

20x1				
Dec.	3			
20x2				
Mar.	17			
May	31			
June	10			
	30			
		Accrual of interest on U.S. Treasury bills		
		x / 120 =		
	30			
		Recognition of unrealized gain on trading portfolio:		

Security	Cost	Market Value	
Sun's Fruit, Inc. (12,000 shares)			
Bytes, Inc. (15,000 shares)			
Totals			
Credit balance of Allowance to Adjust Short-Term Investments from 20x1			
Excess of cost over market value in 20x2			
Total adjustment			

2. **Balance sheet presentation shown**

Security	Cost	

Chapter 9, P 6.

1. T accounts prepared and data entered

Accounts Receivable

Allowance for Uncollectible Accounts

2. Uncollectible Accounts Expense and ending balance of Allowance for Uncollectible Accounts determined

a. Percentage of net sales method:

Uncollectible Accounts Expense	=			x		
	=	0.025	x	(	−	)
	=					
Allowance for Uncollectible Accounts	=		+		−	
	=					
Accounts Receivable, Net	=		−			
	=					

b. Accounts receivable aging method:

Uncollectible Accounts Expense	=		+	
	=			
Allowance for Uncollectible Accounts	=			
Accounts Receivable, Net	=		−	
	=			

Chapter 9, P 6. (Continued)

3. Receivable turnover and average days' sales uncollected calculated

Receivable Turnover =

(___ * + ___ **) ÷ ___

= ___ = ___ times

Average Days' Sales Uncollected = ___ days / ___ = ___ days[†]

* ___ − ___ = ___

** ___ − ___ = ___

[†] Rounded.

4. Difference in methods and rationales discussed

1. Aging analysis completed

Forsell Fashions Store
Aging Analysis of Accounts Receivable
January 31, 20x2

Customer Account	Total	Not Yet Due	1–30 Days Past Due	31–60 Days Past Due	61–90 Days Past Due	Over 90 Days Past Due
Balance Forward						

2. End-of-year balances computed

Accounts Receivable		

Allowance for Uncollectible Accounts		

3. Analysis of estimated uncollectible accounts prepared

Forsell Fashions Store
Estimated Uncollectible Accounts
January 31, 20x2

	Amount	Percentage Considered Uncollectible	Allowance for Uncollectible Accounts

4. Entry in journal form for uncollectible accounts expense prepared

20x2					
Jan.	31				
			To record estimated uncollectible accounts expense:		
			Desired balance		
			Debit balance in allowance account		
			Amount of adjustment		

Chapter 9, P 8.

20xx									
Jan.	14								
Feb.	13								
May	14								
			Received payment from Riordan						
			Company for note and interest						
				x		/ 100	x	/ 360	
			=						
	15								
July	14								
			Calvin Eng Company dishonored note						
				x	/	x	/		
			=						

20xx										
July	20									
			Collection on account from Calvin Eng Company, including 12 percent interest for six days							
				x		/ 100	x		/ 360	
		=								
	25									
	31									
Sept	14									
			Leona Fancy Company dishonored note							
				x	/		x	/		
		=								
	25									

1. Investment transactions recorded

Jan.	10							
Feb.	10							
			Receipt of dividends on stock investments					
			Ford:					
				shares x	$0.50	=		
			McDonald's:					
				shares x		=		
			IBM:					
				shares x		=		
			Total					
Apr.	10							
May	10							

June	1					
			Sale of 500 shares of McDonald's at $55:			
			shares x $55.00 =			
			shares x =			
			Gain			
	30					
			To adjust for decline in market value			
			of stock investments			
				Market	Cost	Gain (Loss)
			Ford (1,000 shares)			
			McDonald's (2,000 shares)			
			IBM (2,100 shares)			
			Total			
Aug.	10					
			Receipt of dividends on stock investments			
			Ford:			
			shares x =			
			McDonald's:			
			shares x =			
			IBM:			
			shares x =			
			Total			

Chapter 9, SD 6. (Continued)

Nov.	1					
			Sale of short-term investments:			
				Selling Price	Cost	Gain (Loss) on Sale
			Ford (1,000 shares)			
			McDonald's (2,000 shares)			
			IBM (2,100 shares)			
			Total			

2.	Balance sheet presentation on June 30 shown

Short-Term Investments (at market, cost is $454,500)	

3.	Allowance account discussed

4.	Strategy assessed

1. Ratios computed (dollar amounts in thousands)

		2001	2000	1999
Ratio of Uncollectible Accounts Expense				
	To Net Sales*	=	=	=
	To Accounts Receivable	=	=	=
Ratio of Allowance for Uncollectible Accounts				
	To Accounts Receivable	=	=	=

*Two decimal places needed to show any difference.

2. Ratios calculated (dollar amounts in thousands)

Receivable Turnover	=	

(Note: The net accounts receivable need to be calculated for 2001, 2000, and 1999.)

2001	=	(_____ + _____) ÷

	=	_____ = _____ times

2000	=	(_____ + _____) ÷

	=	_____ = _____ times

1999	=	(_____ + _____) ÷

	=	_____ = _____ times

Average Days' Sales Uncollected	=	

2001	=	$\dfrac{365}{\ \ }$ = _____ days*

2000	=	_____ = _____ days*

1999	=	_____ = _____ days*

*Rounded.

3. **Interpretation of ratios**

1.   Cash and cash equivalents discussed

2.   Allowance for Uncollectible Accounts discussed

3. Quick ratios computed and discussed (in millions)

Quick Ratio	=		
2000:		+	
	=	=	
1999:		+	
	=	=	

4. **Receivable ratios computed and discussed (in millions)**

Receivable Turnover =					
2000:	(	+	) ÷		
=		=	**times**		
1999:	(	+	) ÷		
=		=	**times**		
Average Days' Sales Uncollected =					
2000:	$\dfrac{365}{}$	=	**days**		
1999:		=	**days**		

Chapter 10, SE 1.

1.		3.		
2.		4.		

Chapter 10, SE 2.

Inventory Turnover	=	

	=	
		(+) ÷

	=		=	times

Average Days' Inventory on Hand	=	

	=	days / times	=	days

Chapter 10, SE 3.

Specific identification method:

Goods available for sale				
Less ending inventory				
From August 8 purchase	(	units x	)	
From August 22 purchase	(	units x	)	
Cost of goods sold				

Chapter 10, SE 4.

Average-cost method—periodic inventory system:

Goods available for sale			
Less ending inventory			
Average cost times units on hand			
* x units =			**
Cost of goods sold			
* ÷ units =			
** Rounded.			

Chapter 10, SE 5.

FIFO method—periodic inventory system:

Goods available for sale							
Less ending inventory							
From August 22 purchase	(		**units**	x		)	
From August 8 purchase	(		**units**	x		)	
Cost of goods sold							

Chapter 10, SE 6.

LIFO method—periodic inventory system:

Goods available for sale							
Less ending inventory							
From beginning inventory	(		**units**	x		)	
From August 8 purchase	(		**units**	x		)	
Cost of goods sold							

Average-cost method—perpetual inventory system:

			Units	Cost per Unit*	Amount*
Aug.	1	Inventory			
	8	Purchase			
	8	Balance			
	15	Sale			
	15	Balance			
	22	Purchase			
	22	Balance			
	28	Sale			
	31	Inventory			
Cost of goods sold			(	+	)

*Rounded.

Chapter 10, SE 8.

FIFO method—perpetual inventory system:

			Units	Cost per Unit		
Aug.	1					
	8					
	8					
	15					
	15					
	22					
	22					
	28					
	31					
Cost of goods sold			(	+	)	

Chapter 10, SE 9.

LIFO method—perpetual inventory system:

			Units	Cost per Unit		
Aug.	1					
	8					
	8					
	15					
	15					
	22					
	22					
	28					
	31					
Cost of goods sold			(	+	)	

	Periodic Inventory System				Perpetual Inventory System		
	Specific Identification Method	Average-Cost Method	FIFO Method	LIFO Method	Average-Cost Method	FIFO Method	LIFO Method
Ending inventory							
Cost of goods sold							

Chapter 10, SE 11.

Item	Quantity	Cost per Unit	Market per Unit	Cost	Market	Item-by-Item
Short sleeve						
Long sleeve						
Extra-long sleeve						

Lower of cost or market on an item-by-item basis is

Lower of cost or market on a major category basis is

Chapter 10, E 1.

1.	
2.	
3.	
4.	
5.	
6.	

Chapter 10, E 2.

Inventory Turnover	=					
20x2:	=	(	+	) ÷		
	=		=	**times**		
20x3:	=	(	+	) ÷		
	=		=	**times**		
Average Days' Inventory on Hand	=					
20x2:	=	days / times	=	**days**		
20x3:	=	days / times	=	**days**		

Chapter 10, E 3.

1. Inventory costs assigned by the specific identification method

June	15	Purchase,		cases	@			
Jan.	1	Inventory,		cases	@			
Oct.	15	Purchase,		cases	@			
Dec.	15	Purchase,		cases	@			
Cost of goods sold								
Ending inventory								
		–			=			

2. Inventory costs assigned by the average-cost method

Average unit cost:			÷	units =		
Cost of goods available for sale						
Less Dec. 31 inventory						
	cases x					
Cost of goods sold						

3. Inventory costs assigned by the FIFO method

Cost of goods available for sale				
Less Dec. 31 inventory				
	cases @		from Dec. 15 purchase	
	cases @		from Oct. 15 purchase	
	cases			
Cost of goods sold				

4. Inventory costs assigned by the LIFO method

Cost of goods available for sale				
Less Dec. 31 inventory				
	cases @		from Jan. 1 inventory	
	cases @		from Feb. 25 purchase	
	cases			
Cost of goods sold				

Chapter 10, E 3. (Continued)

Chapter 10, E 4.

1.	Cost of goods sold computed by FIFO method

	Year 1	Year 2	Year 3

2.	Cost of goods sold computed by LIFO method

	Year 1	Year 2	Year 3

Chapter 10, E 5.

Sales		units x				
		units x				
		units x				
		units x				
		units x				
		units				
Beginning inventory		units x				
Purchases		units x				
		units x				
		units x				
Cost of goods available						
for sale		units				

Periodic inventory system—average-cost method:

Sales						
Cost of goods sold						
Cost of goods available for sale						
Less ending inventory	(	units x		*)		
Cost of goods sold						
Gross margin						
*	÷	units =		(rounded)		

Periodic inventory system—FIFO method:

Sales				
Cost of goods sold				
Cost of goods available for sale				
Less ending inventory			*	
Cost of goods sold				
Gross margin				
*	units x		=	

Periodic inventory system—LIFO method:

			*	
Sales				
Cost of goods sold				
Cost of goods available for sale				
Less ending inventory			*	
Cost of goods sold				
Gross margin				

*		**units**	X		=	
		units	X		=	

Chapter 10, E 6.

Perpetual inventory system—average-cost method

Date			Units	Cost*	Amount
June	1	Inventory			
	4	Purchase			
	4	Balance			
	8	Sale			
	8	Balance			
	12	Purchase			
	12	Balance			
	16	Sale			
	20	Sale			
	20	Balance			
	24	Purchase			
	24	Balance			
	28	Sale			
	28	Balance			
	29	Sale			
	30	Inventory			

*Rounded.

Sales	
Cost of goods sold	
Gross margin	

Computations:

	Sales	Cost of Goods Sold
Total		

Perpetual inventory system—FIFO method

Date			Units	Cost	Amount
June	1	Inventory			
	4	Purchase			
	4	Balance			
	8	Sale			
	8	Balance			
	12	Purchase			
	12	Balance			
	16	Sale			
	16	Balance			
	20	Sale			
	20	Balance			
	24	Purchase			
	24	Balance			
	28	Sale			
	28	Balance			
	29	Sale			
	30	Inventory			

Sales		
Cost of goods sold		
Gross margin		

Computations:

	Sales	Cost of Goods Sold
Total		

Perpetual inventory system—LIFO method

Date			Units	Cost	Amount
June	1	Inventory			
	4	Purchase			
	4	Balance			
	8	Sale			
	8	Balance			
	12	Purchase			
	12	Balance			
	16	Sale			
	16	Balance			
	20	Sale			
	20	Balance			
	24	Purchase			
	24	Balance			
	28	Sale			
	28	Balance			
	29	Sale			
	30	Inventory			

Chapter 10, E 6. (Continued)

Sales	
Cost of goods sold	
Gross margin	

Computations:

	Sales	Cost of Goods Sold
Total		

Chapter 10, E 7.

Cost of goods available for sale and ending inventory in units

	Units	Cost	Total
Beginning inventory			
Purchase 1			
Purchase 2			
Purchase 3			
Purchase 4			
Purchase 5			
Cost of goods available for sale			
Sale in units			
Ending inventory in units			

1. Periodic inventory system

a. Specific identification method:

Sales			
Cost of goods available for sale			
Less ending inventory		*	
Cost of goods sold			
Gross margin			

* Purchase 1	units	X		
Purchase 2	units	X		
Purchase 5	units	X		

b. Average-cost method:

Sales			
Cost of goods available for sale			
Less ending inventory		*	
Cost of goods sold			
Gross margin			

* Average cost =		+		=	
	X		units	=	

c. FIFO method:

Sales			
Cost of goods available for sale			
Less ending inventory		*	
Cost of goods sold			
Gross margin			

* Purchase 5	units	X		
Purchase 4	units	X		
Purchase 3	units	X		

Chapter 10, E 7. (Continued)

d. LIFO method:

Sales			
Cost of goods available for sale			
Less ending inventory			*
Cost of goods sold			
Gross margin			

* Beginning inventory		units	x		
Purchase 1		units	x		
Purchase 2		units	x		

2. Perpetual inventory system

a. Average-cost method:

Sales			
Cost of goods sold			*
Gross margin			

	Units	Cost	Amount
Beginning inventory			
Purchase 1			
Balance			
Sale 1			
Balance			
Purchase 2			
Balance			
Purchase 3			
Balance			
Purchase 4			
Balance			
Sale 2			
Balance			
Purchase 5			
Ending inventory			

* Cost of goods sold =	+		=	

b. <u>FIFO method:</u>

Sales			
Cost of goods sold			*
Gross margin			

*	**Sale 1**	**From Beginning inventory**	**units**	
	Sale 2	**From Purchase 1**	**units**	
		From Purchase 2	**units**	
		From Purchase 3	**units**	
	Cost of goods sold		**units**	

Ending inventory =   −   =

c. <u>LIFO method:</u>

Sales			
Cost of goods sold			*
Gross margin			

*	**Sale 1**	**From Purchase 1**	**units**	
		From Beginning inventory	**units**	
	Sale 2	**From Purchase 4**	**units**	
		From Purchase 3	**units**	
	Cost of goods sold		**units**	

Ending inventory =   −   =

Chapter 10, E 8.

								FIFO Method	LIFO Method
Sales (		x		)					
Cost of Goods Sold									
Beginning Inventory:									
		x							
Purchases									
		x							
		x							
Goods Available for Sale									
Less Ending Inventory									
FIFO (		x		)					
LIFO (		x		)					
Cost of Goods Sold									
Gross Margin									
Operating Expenses									
Income Before Income Taxes									
Income Taxes									
Net Income									

If a year-end purchase of 10,000 cases at $30 per case is made, the following will result:

	FIFO Method	LIFO Method
Sales (x)		
Cost of Goods Sold		
Beginning Inventory:		
x		
Purchases		
x		
x		
x		
Goods Available for Sale		
Less Ending Inventory		
FIFO (x)		
LIFO (x)		
Cost of Goods Sold		
Gross Margin		
Operating Expenses		
Income Before Income Taxes		
Income Taxes		
Net Income		

Chapter 10, E 9.

1.		6.	
2.		7.	
3.		8.	
4.		9.	
5.		10.	

Chapter 10, E 10.

	20x4	20x3

Chapter 10, E 11.

1. Lower-of-cost-or-market value computed, using the item-by-item method

	Quantity	Per Unit Cost	Per Unit Market	Lower of Cost or Market
Category I				
Item aa	200	$ 2.00	$ 1.80	
Item bb	240	4.00	4.40	
Item cc	400	8.00	7.50	
Category II				
Item dd	300	12.00	13.00	
Item ee	400	18.00	18.20	
Inventory at the lower of cost or market				

2. Lower-of-cost-or-market value computed, using the major category method

	Quantity	Per Unit Cost	Per Unit Market	Total Cost	Total Market	Lower of Cost or Market
Category I						
Item aa	200	$ 2.00	$ 1.80			
Item bb	240	4.00	4.40			
Item cc	400	8.00	7.50			
Totals						
Category II						
Item dd	300	12.00	13.00			
Item ee	400	18.00	18.20			
Totals						
Inventory at the lower of cost or market						

Chapter 10, E 12.

1. Ending inventory estimated by retail method

	Cost	Retail
Beginning inventory		
Ratio of cost to retail price: ———— =		

2. Loss estimated

Chapter 10, E 13.

Chapter 10, P 1.

1. Schedule of cost of goods available for sale prepared

	Units	Price	Total Cost
Beginning inventory			
Purchases			
Cost of goods available for sale			

2. Income before income taxes computed

a. Average-cost method:

Sales (	x	)		

b. FIFO method:

c. LIFO method:

3. Ratios computed

	Average-Cost			FIFO			LIFO		
Cost of goods sold	(	+	) ÷	(	+	) ÷	(	+	) ÷
Average inventory									
Inventory turnover	(	÷	) times	(	÷	) times	(	÷	) times
Average days'		days			days			days	
inventory on hand	(days	÷	times)	(days	÷	times)	(days	÷	times)

1. Periodic inventory system—average-cost method

	Units	Unit Price	Amount
June 1 Beginning inventory			
June 30 Ending inventory			
July 1 Beginning inventory			

	Units	Unit Price	Amount
Purchases			
July 2			

July 31 Ending inventory			

2.   Periodic inventory system—FIFO method

	Units	Unit Price	Amount
June 1 Beginning inventory			
June 30 Ending inventory			*

*From purchase on June 10.

July 1 Beginning inventory

	Units	Unit Price	Amount	Units	Unit Price	Amount
Purchases						
July 2						
July 31 Ending inventory						*

*	July 22 Purchase	(	units	X	)	
	July 14 Purchase	(	units	X	)	
	Total					

3. Periodic inventory system—LIFO method

	Units	Unit Price	Amount
June 1 Beginning inventory			
June 30 Ending inventory			*

***June 1 Beginning inventory**		
(units x)		
June 10 Purchase		
(units x)		
Total		

July 1 Beginning inventory

	Units	Unit Price	Amount				
Purchases							
July 2							
July 31 Ending inventory							*

***June 1 Beginning inventory**		
(units x)		
June 10 Purchase		
(units x)		
July 2 Purchase		
(units x)		
Total		

Chapter 10, P 3.

1. Perpetual inventory system—average-cost method

Date			Units	Cost	Amount
June	1				
	5				
	5				
	10				
	10				
	17				
	30				
July	2				
	2				
	8				
	8				
	14				
	14				
	18				
	18				
	22				
	22				
	26				
	26				
	30				
	31				

2. Perpetual inventory system—FIFO method

Date			Units	Cost	Amount
June	1				
	5				
	5				
	10				
	10				
	17				
	30				
July	2				
	2				
	8				
	8				
	14				
	14				
	18				
	18				
	22				
	22				
	26				
	26				
	30				
	31				

3. | **Perpetual inventory system—LIFO method**

Date			Units	Cost	Amount
June	1				
	5				
	5				
	10				
	10				
	17				
	30				
July	2				
	2				
	8				
	8				
	14				
	14				
	18				
	18				
	22				
	22				
	26				
	26				
	30				
	31				

Chapter 10, P 3. (Continued)

Chapter 10, P 4.

	Cost	Retail
1. Beginning inventory		
Ratio of cost to retail price: ——— =		
Estimated cost of ending inventory		
x =		
2. July 31 Physical inventory		
x =		
3. Estimated inventory shortage at cost and retail		

Brandon Oil Products
Schedule to Estimate Inventory Destroyed
April 27, 20xx

Beginning Inventory at Cost		

Chapter 10, P 6.

1. Schedule of cost of goods available for sale prepared

	Units	Price	Total Cost

2. Income before income taxes computed

a. Average-cost method:

Sales (	x	)		

b. <u>FIFO method:</u>

c. <u>LIFO method:</u>

Chapter 10, P 6. (Continued)

3. Ratios computed

	Average-Cost	FIFO	LIFO
Cost of goods sold			
Average inventory	( ) ÷	( ) ÷	( ) ÷
	( )	( )	( )
Inventory turnover	÷ times	÷ times	÷ times
	( )	( )	( )
Average days'	days	days	days
inventory on hand	(days ÷ times)	(days ÷ times)	(days ÷ times)

1. Periodic inventory system—average-cost method

	Units	Unit Price	Amount
Cost of goods available for sale			
Mar. 31 Ending inventory			
Apr. 1 Beginning inventory			

	Units	Unit Price	Amount			
Purchases						
Apr. 4						

2. Periodic inventory system—FIFO method

	Units	Unit Price	Amount
Mar. 31 Ending inventory			*

*From purchase on Mar. 10.

Apr. 1 Beginning inventory

	Units	Unit Price	Amount			
Purchases						
Apr. 4						
Apr. 30 Ending inventory						*

*From purchase on Apr. 25.

3. Periodic inventory system—LIFO method

	Units	Unit Price	Amount
Mar. 31 Ending inventory			*

*Mar. 1 Beginning inventory

(units x   )

Mar. 10 Purchase

(units x   )

Apr. 1 Beginning inventory

	Units	Unit Price	Amount			
Purchases						
Apr. 4						
Apr. 30 Ending inventory						*

*From Mar. 1 inventory.

Chapter 10, P 8.

1. Perpetual inventory system—average-cost method

Date			Units	Cost	Amount
Mar.	1				
	7				
	7				
	10				
	10				
	19				
	31				
Apr.	4				
	4				
	11				
	11				
	15				
	15				
	23				
	23				
	25				
	25				
	27				
	30				

2. Perpetual inventory system—FIFO method

Date		Units	Cost	Amount
Mar.	1			
	7			
	7			
	10			
	10			
	19			
	31			
Apr.	4			
	4			
	11			
	11			
	15			
	15			
	23			
	23			
	25			
	25			
	27			
	30			

3. Perpetual inventory system—LIFO method

Date			Units	Cost	Amount
Mar.	1				
	7				
	7				
	10				
	10				
	19				
	31				
Apr.	4				
	4				
	11				
	11				
	15				
	15				
	23				
	23				
	25				
	25				
	27				
	30				

FIFO and LIFO methods with purchase compared

				FIFO Method	LIFO Method
Sales (		units	x	)		
Cost of Goods Sold					
Purchases					
		x			
		x			
		x			
Total Purchases					
Less Ending Inventory					
FIFO:		x			
		x			
LIFO:		x			

Chapter 10, SD 5. (Continued)

Comparison of cash outcomes and recommendation of inventory system

Memorandum

Date:

To:

From:

Re:

	Cash Flows, Option 1		Cash Flows, Option 2	
	FIFO	LIFO	FIFO	LIFO
Sales				
Purchases				
Operating Expenses				
Income Taxes				
Cash Flows				

Discussion:

Recommendations:

Inventory Turnover*	=					
Pioneer	=					
		(		+		) ÷
	=			=		times
Yamaha	=					
		(		+		) ÷
	=			=		times

*Amounts are in millions.

Average Days' Inventory on Hand	=				
Pioneer	=	days / times	=		days
Yamaha	=	days / times	=		days

Inventory Turnover*	=			
1999	=	(.	+	) ÷
	=		=	**times**
2000	=	(	+	) ÷
	=		=	**times**

*Amounts are in millions.

Average Days' Inventory on Hand	=			
1999	=	days / times	=	days
2000	=	days / times	=	days

Chapter 11, SE 1.

1.		4.	
2.		5.	
3.			

Chapter 11, SE 2.

1.		5.	
2.		6.	
3.		7.	
4.		8.	

Chapter 11, SE 3.

Asset	Appraisal	Percentage	Apportionment	
Total				

Chapter 11, SE 4.

Depreciation for each year:

(−   ) ÷   years =

Chapter 11, SE 5.

Depreciation for

Year 1: (−   ) x —————— =

Year 2: (−   ) x —————— =

Year 3: (−   ) x —————— =

Year 4: (−   ) x —————— =

Chapter 11, SE 6.

Depreciation for

Year 1:					x	50%	=			
Year 2: (		–		)	x		=			
Year 3: (		–		)	x		=			
Year 4:		–			*	=			**	

*		+		+		=	

** Remaining amount to reduce to salvage value:

	–		(salvage value)	=	

Chapter 11, SE 7.

1.	Jan.	4			
2.	Jan.	4			
3.	Jan.	4			

Chapter 11, SE 8.

1.	Jan.	4				
2.	Jan.	4				
3.	Jan.	4				

Chapter 11, SE 9.

Depletion charge per ton:

(−   ) ÷   tons =   per ton

Depletion expense for the first year:

     tons x   =

Depreciation expense for the first year:

     x (tons ÷   tons) =

Chapter 11, SE 10.

Intangible Assets

Software		*

*   − (÷   years)

Chapter 11, E 1.

1.		4.	
2.		5.	
3.		6.	

Chapter 11, E 2.

Management should purchase the new machine because

			Present Value
Acquisition cost			
Present value factor	=		
	x		
Net annual cash flows			
Present value factor	=		
(Table 4: 5 periods,	9%	)	
	x		
Disposal price			
Present value factor	=		
(Table 3: 5 periods,		)	
	x		
Net present value			

Chapter 11, E 3.

Cost of land:

Total cost of land	

Cost of land improvements:

Total cost of land improvements	

Chapter 11, E 4.

Asset	Value	Percentage	Apportionment*	

* Land		X		=	
Building		X		=	
Equipment		X		=	

Chapter 11, E 5.

Cost and depreciable cost of tractor:

First year's depreciation:

		÷		=	

Chapter 11, E 6.

1. Depreciation computed by straight-line method:

	/		x		=	

2. Depreciation computed by production method:

		÷		x		=	

3. Depreciation computed by double-declining-balance method:

20x4	0.40	x			=			
20x5		x	(		–		) =	
			x			=		

Adjusting entry:

Balance sheet presentation:

Chapter 11, E 7.

Year 1	0.50	x		=										
Year 2		x	(	−	)	=	0.50	x		=				
Year 3		x	(	−	)	=		x		=				
Year 4		−	**Estimated Residual Value**	=		−		=						

Chapter 11, E 8.

1.	Jan.	2			
2.	Jan.	2			
3.	Jan.	2			
4.	Jan.	2			
5.	Jan.	2			
6.	Jan.	2			

	20x4										
	July	1									
				To record one-half year's depreciation							
				on computer							
				(		–		)	÷	years	
					x		/	12	=		
1.	20x4										
	July	1									
				Computer discarded after 3 1/2 years							
					years	x		=			
2.	20x4										
	July	1									
3.	20x4										
	July	1									
4.	20x4										
	July	1									

5.	20x4					
	July	1				
6.	20x4					
	July	1				
7.	20x4					
	July	1				
8.	20x4					
	July	1				
9.	20x4					
	July	1				

Chapter 11, E 10.

1. Depletion charge per ton computed

Estimated tons of ore	÷	10,000,000

2. Depletion expense computed

Depletion charge per ton	X		

3. Depreciation expense determined for buildings

Cost of buildings			
Percentage of depletion			
(— ÷ —)	X		
Depreciation expense			

4. **Depreciation expense determined for equipment**

Cost of equipment				
Percentage of depletion		x		
a.	Depreciation proportional to depletion			
b.	Depreciation, straight-line method			
	(+ years)			

Chapter 11, E 11.

1. Cost of copyright	
2. Cost of trademark	

Chapter 11, E 12.

Cost	
Less estimated residual value	
Depreciable cost	
1. Depreciation computed by straight-line method:	
2. Depreciation computed by production method:	
3. Depreciation computed by double-declining-balance method:	

Chapter 11, E 13.

Cost	
Residual value	
Depreciable cost	

First-year depreciation:

Second-year depreciation:

Remaining depreciable cost:

Remaining useful life:

Third-year depreciation:

Chapter 11, E 14.

1.	
2.	
3.	
4.	
5.	
6.	

Chapter 11, E 15.

1. Entry prepared to record cost of repair

2. Carrying value computed

3. Depreciation entry prepared

	To record depreciation expense						
			÷		years	=	

Oslo Company
Schedule of Proper Charges to Asset and Expense Accounts
December 31, 20xx

	Land	Land Improvements	Buildings	Machinery	Expense
Land					

Chapter 11, P 2.

1. Depreciation computed

Depreciation Table

	Depreciation Method	Year	Computation			Depreciation	Carrying Value
a.	Straight-line	1		x	/		
		2		x	/		
		3		x	/		
		4		x	/		
		5		x	/		
		6		x	/		
b.	Production	1		x	10,000		
		2		x	10,000		
		3		x	10,000		
		4		x	10,000		
		5		x	10,000		
		6		x	10,000		
c.	Double-declining-balance	1		x	/		
		2		x	/		
		3		x	/		
		4		x	/		
		5		x	/		
		6		—			*	

* To reduce to estimated residual value.

2. **Adjusting entry prepared—straight-line method**

3. **Balance sheet presentation after two years shown**

4. **Conclusions drawn from depreciation patterns**

Equipment No.	Computations			Depreciation		
				20x1	20x2	20x3
1	× 0.2					
	(	1	−	)	×	
	(	1	−	)	×	
2	× 0.1	×	/			
	×					
	×					
3	×	÷				
	×	÷				
	×	÷				
Total Depreciation Expense						

a.

b.

c.

d.

e.								
		To record exchange of computer, no gain recognized under APB accounting rules						
			−		=			
f.								
g.								
		To record exchange of computers, no gain recognized under income tax rules						
			−		=			
h.								
		To record exchange of computers, no loss recognized under income tax rules						
			+		=			

Part A.   Journal entries prepared

a.					
b.					
c.					
		Purchase of leasehold improvements			
d.					
		Amortization of leasehold for one year			
		÷	years	=	
e.					
		Amortization of leasehold improvements for one year			
		÷	years	=	

Part B.   Journal entries prepared

a.				
b.				
c.				
		Amortization of patent for one year		
		÷	years	
	=			
d.				
		Write-off of patent as worthless		
		− (	x)	
	=			

471

Georgakis Computers
Schedule of Proper Charges for Training Center
December 31, 20x2

	Land	Land Improvements	Building	Equipment
Attorney's fee				

Chapter 11, P 7.

1. **Depreciation computed**

Depreciation Table

	Depreciation Method	Year	Computation				Depreciation	Carrying Value
a.	Straight-line	1		x	1 / 4			
		2		x	/			
		3		x	/			
		4		x	/			
b.	Production	1		x	20,000			
		2		x	_____			
		3		x	_____			
		4	—	x	_____			
c.	Double-	1		x	0.5			
	declining-	2		x				
	balance	3		x				
		4		—			*	

*Maximum depreciation allowed in last year.

2. **Adjusting entry prepared—straight-line method**

3. **Balance sheet presentation after two years shown**

4. **Conclusions drawn from depreciation patterns**

Chapter 11, P 8.

Asset	Computations							Depreciation 20x2	20x3	20x4
Washing machines	$28,800	x	/ 4	x	/ 12					
		x	/							
		x	/							
Tanning machine	7,500	x								
		x								
		x								
Refreshment center		x	0.2	x	3	/	12			
	(	x		x		/		) +		
	(	x		x		/		)		
	(	x		x		/		) +		
	(	x		x		/		)		
Total Depreciation Expense										

Chapter 11, SD 6.

1.   Present value computed for each type of equipment

Type A

| | Immediate Cash Outlay = Present Value |

Type B

Amount of Non-Interest-Bearing Note x **Factor** = **Present Value**

| | x | | = | | (factor from Table 3 in the appendix |

on future value and present value tables = 2 years at 16 percent)

2.   Net present value computed for each type of equipment

Type A

Annual Net Cash Receipts x **Factor** = **Present Value**

| | x | | = | | (factor from Table 4 in the appendix |

on future value and present value tables = 5 years at 16 percent)

| | Net Present Value = | | − | | = | |

Type B

	Net Cash Receipts	x	Factor*	=	Present Value
Year 1		x		=	
Year 2		x	0.743	=	
Year 3		x		=	
Year 4		x		=	
Year 5		x		=	
Total present value					
Net Present Value =		−		=	

*Table 3 in the same appendix, 16%.

3. | **Memorandum with recommendation**

| **Memorandum** |
| Date: |
| To: |
| From: |
| Re: |

We have two machines that will enable us to manufacture the parts for our new subcontract:

	Option A:
	Option B:

Chapter 12, SE 1.

1.		3.		5.	
2.		4.			

Chapter 12, SE 2.

Working Capital	=				
	=		−		=

Payables Turnover =

$$= \frac{+}{(\quad + \quad) \div}$$

	=		=	times

Average Days' Payable	=		=	days	=	days

Chapter 12, SE 3.

1.		4.	
2.		5.	
3.		6.	

Chapter 12, SE 4.

1.	Aug.	31			
2.	Oct.	30			
			Payment of note plus interest		
			x	x	÷ 360	
			=		

Chapter 12, SE 5.

1.	**Aug.**	**31**				
2.	**Oct.**	**30**				
	30					

Chapter 12, SE 6.

1.	**Apr.**	**30**				
2.	**Apr.**	**30**				
			To record payroll expenses			
				+	=	
				−	=	
				x	=	
				x	=	

Chapter 12, SE 7.

Oct.	**31**					
			To record estimated product warranty expense, calculated as follows:			
			Number of units sold			
			Rate of replacement	x		
			Estimated units to be replaced			
			Estimated cost per unit	x		
			Estimated liability			
	31					
			To record replacement of clocks			
			under warranty (clocks	x	**)**	

Chapter 12, SE 8.

Vacation pay expense for September:

(		−		)	×	.7	×		*	=	

*		÷		=				

Chapter 12, SE 9.

	Taxes Paid by Employees	Taxes Paid by Employer

Chapter 12, SE 10.

	Taxes Paid by Employees	Taxes Paid by Employer

Chapter 12, E 1.

1.		4.		7.	
2.		5.		8.	
3.		6.			

Chapter 12, E 2.

20x1:

Working Capital	=				
	=		−		=
Payables Turnover	=				
	=		+		
		(	+	) ÷ 2	
	=		= times		
Average Days' Payable	=		=	365 days	= days

20x2:

Working Capital	=				
	=		−		=
Payables Turnover	=				
	=		−		
		(	+	) +	
	=		= times		
Average Days' Payable	=		=	365 days	= days

Chapter 12, E 3.

1.	Oct.	31				
2.	Nov.	30				
3.	Dec.	30				

Chapter 12, E 4.

1.	Oct.	31				
2.	Nov.	30				
3.	Dec.	30				
		30				

Chapter 12, E 5.

1. Amount of revenue determined

Revenue for the month:		+		=	

2. Entry in journal form prepared

Aug.	31				

Chapter 12, E 6.

1.	Oct.	31			
2.	Oct.	31			
			To record payroll expenses		
			÷	0.20	=
			−		=
		0.008	×		=
			×		=

Chapter 12, E 7.

1. Estimated liability recorded

July	31					
		To record estimated product warranty expense, calculated as follows:				
		Number of units sold				
		Rate of replacement	x	_____		
		Estimated units to be replaced				
		Estimated cost per unit	x	_____		
		Estimated liability				

2. Games' replacement recorded

July	31					
		To record replacement of games under warranty				
		(games x)				

Chapter 12, E 8.

1. Employee benefit for July vacation estimated

(_____ – _____) x _____ x 3 ÷ _____ = _____

2 and 3. Entries in journal form prepared

July	31					
	31					

Chapter 12, E 9.

20x1							
July	31						
			To record estimated property tax expense for the month				
			(x 1.08) ÷ months				
			=				
Aug.	31						
Sept.	30						
			To record estimated property tax expense for the month, including adjustment for previous two months				
			÷ =				
			+ (x *) =				
		*	− =				
Oct.	31						
Nov.	1						
	30						

Chapter 12, E 10.

1. Schedule of employee earnings prepared

		Muzzy Company		
		Schedule of Wages Subject to Payroll Taxes		
Employee Name	Cumulative Earnings	Earnings Subject to Social Security Tax	Earnings Subject to Medicare Tax	Earnings Subject to Unemployment Taxes

2. Social security, Medicare, and unemployment taxes computed

Social security tax				
Employees' share:		x	0.062	
Employer's share:		x		
Total social security tax				
Medicare tax				
Employees' share:		x		
Employer's share:		x		
Total Medicare tax				
State unemployment tax				
	x			
Federal unemployment tax				
	x			

Chapter 12, E 11.

1. Employee's net pay computed

a.	Total pay							
	Regular time:		hours	x				
	Overtime:		hours	x		x	1.5	
	Total pay							
b.	Federal income taxes withheld:							
c.	Social security tax:	0.062		x		=		
	Medicare tax:			x		=		
d.	Net pay							
	Total pay							
	Less:							
	Net pay							

2. Entry in journal form prepared

20xx					
July	11				

1. **Entry in journal form summarizing employee's pay prepared**

		Payroll for year						
			x	0.062	=			
			x		=			

2. **Entry in journal form for payroll expenses prepared**

		Payroll taxes for one year						
			÷	0.20	=			
			−		=			
			x	0.008	=			
			x		=			

3. **Cost of employee determined**

1. Current liabilities determined

The current liabilities of Highland Television Repair as of December 31, 20x0, are as follows:

Accounts Payable					
Notes Payable					
Property Tax Liability					
Sales Tax Payable					
(		x		)	
Social Security Tax Payable					
(		x	0.062	x	2)
Medicare Tax Payable					
(		x		x	)
State Unemployment Tax Payable					
(		x		)	
Federal Unemployment Tax Payable					
(		x		)	
Federal Income Tax Withholding					
Total Current Liabilities					

2. Additional information identified

3. **Liquidity ratios computed and evaluated (cents omitted)**

Working Capital	=					
	=		−		=	

Payables Turnover	=	

	=		+	

	=		=		times

Average Days' Payable	=			=	days	=	days

Entries in journal form prepared

May	**11**				
	21				
June	**30**				
		To accrue interest expense at end of year			
		x	0.14	x	÷ 360 =
	30				
		To recognize expired discount on note			
		x		÷ 90 =	
July	**20**				
Aug.	**9**				
	9				
		To recognize expired discount on note			
		–		=	

Chapter 12, P 3.

1. Entries in journal form prepared

a.	June	30					
b.		30					
			To record estimated warranty expense for June, computed as follows: Washing machines sold x percent expected to require repair x average cost of parts				
				x	0.20	x	
			=				

2. Balance of Estimated Product Warranty Liability account computed

1.–4.   Entries in journal form prepared

1.	Apr.	30			
2.		30			
3.		30			

Payroll taxes expense

0.008	x		=	
	x		=	

4.		30			

1. Payroll register prepared

Payroll Register

Pay Period: November 30

| Employee | Total Hours | Earnings | | | Deductions | | | | Net Pay | Distribution | |
		Regular	Over-time	Gross	Cumulative	Federal Income Taxes	Social Security Tax	Medicare Tax	Supple-mental Benefits Plan		Sales Wages Expense	Adminis-trative Salaries Expense
Epstein, D.	85				5,567.00							

2, 3, and 4. | Entries in journal form prepared

20xx					
Nov.	30				
	30				
			Biweekly payroll taxes expense and employer's contribution to supplemental benefits plan		
			Subject to FUTA tax:		
			Epstein		
			Hladik		
			0.008 x	=	
			x	=	
	30				
	30				

Entries in journal form prepared

20x1												
Nov.	25											
Dec.	16											
	31											
			To accrue interest expense									
				x	0.10	x		÷	360	=		
	31											
			To recognize expired discount on note									
			÷	90	x			=				
20x2												
Jan.	24											
			To record payment of note plus interest for equipment									
				x		x	÷		=			
				—		=						
Mar.	16											
	16											
			To recognize expired discount on note									
				—		=						

Chapter 12, P 7.

1. Entries in journal form prepared

a.	Sept.	30							
			Warranty replacements and						
			related revenue during September						
				units	x		=		
b.		30							
			To record estimated warranty						
			expense for September, computed						
			as follows: Processors sold x percent						
			expected to require replacement x						
			average cost						
					x	0.03	x		=

2. Balance of Estimated Product Warranty Liability account computed

1.–4. **Entries in journal form prepared**

	20xx					
1.	Oct.	31				
2.		31				
3.		31				
			Payroll taxes expense			
			0.008	x	=	
				x	=	
4.		31				

1. The current liabilities of Miller Bicycles as of December 31, 20x1, are as follows:

Accounts Payable	
Notes Payable	
Property Tax Liability	
Sales Tax Payable	
(x)	
Social Security Tax Payable	
(x x 2)	
Medicare Tax Payable	
(x x)	
State Unemployment Tax Payable	
(x)	
Federal Unemployment Tax Payable	
(x)	
Federal Income Tax Withholding	
Total Current Liabilities	

2.

Payables Turnover*	=					
Sun Microsystems	=		−			
	=		=	**times**		
Cisco Systems	=		+			
	=		=	**times**		

*Amounts are in thousands.

Average Days' Payable	=			
Sun Microsystems	=	**times**	=	**days**
Cisco Systems	=	**times**	=	**days**

On January 29, 2000, Toys "R" Us had a payables turnover of _____ times, calculated as follows:

Payables Turnover	=			

	=		+	
		(	+	) ÷

	=			

	=	times		

Average Days' Payable	=		=	days

	=	days		

Chapter 13, SE 1.

1.		4.	
2.		5.	
3.			

Chapter 13, SE 2.

Chapter 13, SE 3.

Computation of capital ratios:

Bob		÷		=	
Kim		÷		=	

Division of income:

Bob		x	=	
Kim		x	=	

Chapter 13, SE 4.

			Bob	Kim	Income Distributed
Total Income for Distribution					
	Distribution of Interest				
		Bob (x 10%)			
		Kim (x)			
Remaining Income After Interest					
	Equal Distribution of Remaining				
		Income			
		Bob			
		Kim			
Remaining Income					
Income of Partners					

Chapter 13, SE 5.

	Bob	Kim	Income Distributed
Total Income for Distribution			
Distribution of Interest			
Bob (X)			
Kim (X)			
Remaining Income After Interest			
Distribution of Salary			
Bob			
Negative Balance After Interest			
and Salary			
Equal Distribution of Remaining			
Income			
Bob			
Kim			
Remaining Income			
Income and Loss of Partners			

Chapter 13, SE 6.

To transfer Kim's Capital account balance to Sonia			

Chapter 13, SE 7.

Partners' equity in the original partnership							
Cash investment by Sonia							
Partners' equity in the new partnership							
Sonia's equity:			x	1	÷	6	
Bonus to original partners							
Investment by Sonia							
Less equity assigned to Sonia							
Distribution of bonus to original partners							
Bob (		x		÷		)	
Kim (		x		÷		)	

New Capital account balances:

Bob		+		=	
Kim		+		=	
Sonia					

Chapter 13, SE 8.

Partners' equity in the original partnership							
Cash investment by Sonia							
Partners' equity in the new partnership							
Sonia's equity:		x		÷	4		
Bonus to new partner							
Equity assigned to Sonia							
Less investment by Sonia							
Distribution of bonus from original partners							
Bob (		x		÷	2	)	
Kim (		x		÷		)	

New Capital account balances:

Bob		−		=	
Kim		−		=	
Sonia					

Chapter 13, SE 9.

Chapter 13, SE 10.

Loss on office equipment computed:

	Bob	Kim
Distribution of Cash to Partners		
Capital Balances		
Distribution of Loss		
Bob (| x ÷ 3)		
Kim (| x ÷)		
Cash to Partners		

1. Computation: The partners share equally.

Samms	(		X		÷	2	) =
Winston	(		X		÷		) =
Total net income							

Note: Because the partnership agreement does not address the distribution of income and losses, the law requires that income and losses be shared equally.

2. Computation: The partners agreed to share the income three-fifths to Samms and two-fifths to Winston.

Samms	(		X		÷	5	) =
Winston	(		X		÷		) =
Total net income							

3. Computation: The partners agreed to share the income in the ratio of their original investments.

Samms	(		X		÷		) =
Winston	(		X		÷		) =
Total net income							

Chapter 13, E 2. (Continued)

| 4. | Computation: | | | | | Income of Partner | | Income |
						Samms	Winston	Distributed
	Total Income for Distribution							
	Distribution of Interest							
		Samms (		x	0.10	)			
		Winston (		x		)			
	Remaining Income After Interest							
	Equal Distribution of Remaining							
	Income							
		Samms (		x	0.50	)			
		Winston (		x		)			
	Remaining Income							
	Income of Partners							

Chapter 13, E 3.

1. Computation:				Income of Partner		Income
				Samms	**Winston**	**Distributed**
Total Income for Distribution						
	Distribution of Salaries					
		Samms				
		Winston				
Remaining Income After Salaries						
	Distribution of Interest					
		Samms (	x	0.06)			
Remaining Income After Salaries						
	and Interest					
		Equal Distribution of Remaining				
		Income				
		Samms (	x	0.50)			
		Winston (	x	)			
Remaining Income						
Income of Partners						

2. Computation:				Income of Partner		Income
				Samms	**Winston**	**Distributed**
Total Income for Distribution						
	Distribution of Salaries					
		Samms				
		Winston				
Remaining Income After Salaries						
	Distribution of Interest					
		Samms (	x	0.06)			
Negative Balance After Salaries						
	and Interest					
		Equal Distribution of Negative				
		Balance				
		Samms (	x	0.50)			
		Winston (	x	)			
Remaining Income						
Income of Partners						

3. Computation:

	Income (Losses) of Partner		Loss Distributed
	Samms	Winston	
Total Loss for Distribution			
Distribution of Salaries			
Samms			
Winston			
Negative Balance After Salaries			
Distribution of Interest			
Samms (___ x 0.06)			
Negative Balance After Salaries			
and Interest			
Equal Distribution of Negative			
Balance			
Samms (___ x 0.50)			
Winston (___ x ___)			
Remaining Loss			
Income and Loss of Partners			

4. Computation:

	Income (Losses) of Partner		Loss Distributed
	Samms	Winston	
Total Loss for Distribution			
Distribution of Salaries			
Samms			
Winston			
Negative Balance After Salaries			
Distribution of Interest			
Samms (___ x 0.06)			
Negative Balance After Salaries			
and Interest			
Equal Distribution of Negative			
Balance			
Samms (___ x 0.50)			
Winston (___ x ___)			
Remaining Loss			
Loss of Partners			

Chapter 13, E 4.

Average capital balances computed

Partner	Date	Capital Balance	x	Months Unchanged	=	Total			Average Capital
Bess	Jan.–Mar.		x		=				
	Apr.–Dec.		x		=				
							÷	12 =	
Crystal	Jan.–Sept.		x		=				
	Oct.–Dec.		x		=				
							÷	=	
						Total average capital			

Average capital balance ratios computed

Bess	=		+		=		*	=	
Crystal	=		+		=		*	=	

*Rounded.

Distribution of income computed

Bess	=		X		=	
Crystal	=		X		=	
		Total income				

Chapter 13, E 5.

1.

Computation:

Original partners' equity		
Hollis's investment		
Total equity of new partnership		
Hollis's equity (x .20)		
Hollis's investment		
Less Hollis's equity		
Bonus to the original partners		*

*Distribution of bonus to original partners:

Elias (	x	1	÷	5)	
Ray (	x		÷	)	
Gerry (	x		÷	)	
			Total bonus		

2.

Computation:					
Original partners' equity					
Hollis's investment					
Total equity of new partnership					
Hollis's equity	(		x	.40)	
Less Hollis's investment					
Bonus to Hollis					*

* **Distribution of bonus from original partners:**					
Elias (		x	÷	5)	
Ray (		x	÷	)	
Gerry (		x	÷	)	
			Total bonus		

Chapter 13, E 6.

Computation:

Cash withdrawn by Hitoshi		
Less Hitoshi's capital		
Bonus to Hitoshi		*

*Distribution of bonus from remaining partners:

Donald (		x		÷	5)	
Sam (		x		÷	)	
				Total bonus		

Chapter 13, E 7.

1. Cash distribution to partners calculated

Phung and Dordek
Statement of Liquidation
December 31, 20xx

Explanation	Cash	Other Assets	Liabilities	Phung, Capital (75%)	Dordek, Capital (25%)	Gain (or Loss) from Realization
Balance						
Sale of Assets						
Payment of Liabilities						
Distribution of Gain (or						*
Loss) from Realization						
Distribution to Partners						

*
Phung (	) x	÷ 4)	
Dordek (	) x	÷)	

2. Entries in journal form prepared

Chapter 13, E 8.

Alice, Meg, and Terry
Statement of Liquidation
July 1, 20x7

Explanation	Cash	Other Assets	Liabilities	Alice, Capital (60%)	Meg, Capital (20%)	Terry, Capital (20%)	Gain (or Loss) from Realization
Balance, July 1, 20x7							

Chapter 13, P 1.

1. Entry in journal form prepared

20x1			

2. Share of income and loss for each partner determined

a. Income and losses shared equally

					20x1	20x2
Chan						
(		x		)		
(		x		)		
Nichols						
(		x		)		
(		x		)		
Totals						

b. Income and losses shared in ratio of 7:3

Chan								
(		x		÷	10	)		
(		x		÷		)		
Nichols								
(		x		÷		)		
(		x		÷		)		
Totals								

c. **Income shared on the basis of the partners' original investments**

							20x1	20x2
Chan								
(		x		÷	150	)		
(		x		÷		)		
Nichols								
(		x		÷		)		
(		x		÷		)		
Totals								

d. **Income and losses shared in the ratio of beginning capital balances**

						20x1	20x2
Chan							
(		x		÷	)		
(		x		÷	)		
Nichols							
(		x		÷	)		
(		x		÷	)		
Totals							

Computation:		
Chan		
	*	
Nichols		
	*	

e. **Interest on investment; remainder shared equally**

20x1 computation:	Loss of Partner		Loss
	Chan	**Nichols**	**Distributed**
Total Loss for Distribution			
Distribution of Interest			
Chan (	x	0.10)		
Nichols (	x	)		
Negative Balance After Interest			
Equal Distribution of Negative			
Balance			
Chan (	x	)		
Nichols (	x	)		
Remaining Loss			
Loss of Partners			

*Share of 20x1 loss

		Income of Partner		Income
		Chan	Nichols	Distributed
	20x2 computation:			
	Total Income for Distribution			
	Distribution of Interest			
	Chan			
	(x)			
	Nichols			
	(x)			
	Remaining Income After Interest			
	Equal Distribution of Remaining			
	Income			
	Chan			
	(x)			
	Nichols			
	(x)			
	Remaining Income			
	Income of Partners			
f.	**Interest and salaries allowed; remainder shared equally**			

		Loss of Partner		Loss
		Chan	Nichols	Distributed
	20x1 computation:			
	Total Loss for Distribution			
	Distribution of Salaries			
	Chan			
	Nichols			
	Negative Balance After Salaries			
	Distribution of Interest			
	Chan (x)			
	Nichols (x)			
	Negative Balance After Salaries			
	and Interest			
	Equal Distribution of Negative			
	Balance			
	Chan (x)			
	Nichols (x)			
	Remaining Loss			
	Loss of Partners			

			Income of Partner		Income
20x2 computation:			**Chan**	**Nichols**	**Distributed**
Total Income for Distribution					
Distribution of Salaries					
Chan					
Nichols					
Remaining Income After Salaries					
Distribution of Interest					
Chan (	x	**)**			
Nichols (	x	**)**			
Remaining Income After Salaries					
and Interest					
Equal Distribution of Remaining					
Income					
Chan (	x	**)**			
Nichols (	x	**)**			
Remaining Income					
Income of Partners					

1. Distribution calculated for income of $272,600

	Income of Partner			Income
	Gregory	Jerome	Owen	Distributed

Chapter 13, P 2. (Continued)

2. Distribution calculated for income of $77,800

| | Income of Partner | | | Income |
	Gregory	Jerome	Owen	Distributed

3. Distribution calculated for $28,400 loss

	Income (Loss) of Partner			Income
	Gregory	Jerome	Owen	Distributed

Chapter 13, P 3.

a.	Nov.	30				

b.	Nov.	30				

c.	Nov.	30				

Computation:

Original partners' capital						
Luke's investment						
Capital of new partnership						
Luke's investment						
Luke's interest (		x		÷	3	)
Bonus to the original partners						*

***Distribution of bonus to original partners:**

Alicia (		x		÷	10	)
Roberta (		x		÷		)
Joanne (		x		÷		)
Total bonus						

d.	Nov.	30					

Computation:

Original partners' capital					
Luke's investment					
Capital of new partnership					
Luke's interest	(		x	÷	3)
Luke's investment					
Bonus to Luke					*

*Distribution of bonus from original partners:

Alicia (		x	÷	10)	
Roberta (		x	÷	)	
Joanne (		x	÷	)	
Total bonus					

e.	Nov.	30					
			Withdrawal of Alicia from the partnership*				

* Absorption by the remaining partners of cash payment in excess of Alicia's capital balance:

Roberta (		x	÷	8)	
Joanne (		x	÷	)	
Total					

f.	Nov.	30					

Chapter 13, P 4.

1. Statement of liquidation prepared

GDL Partnership
Statement of Liquidation
August 31, 20xx

Explanation	Cash	Accounts Receivable	Inventory	Equipment (net)	Accounts Payable	Gary, Capital (50%)	Dawn, Capital (30%)	Leslie, Capital (20%)	Gain (or Loss) from Realization
Balance 8/31/xx									
a.									
b.									
c.									
d.									
e.									
f.									
g.									

Chapter 13, P 4. (Continued)

2.	Entries in journal form prepared		
a.	Aug. 31		
b.	31		
c.	31		
d.	31		
e.	31		
f.	31		
g.	31		

20x1				
Jan.	1			
Dec.	31			

Computation:	Income (Loss) of Partner		Income Distributed
	Flippo	McCovey	

20x2				
Jan.	1			

Computation:

20x2						
Dec.	31					

Computation:	Income of Partner			Income Distributed
	Flippo	McCovey	Stanford	

20x3						
Jan.	1					
	1					
	1					
	1					
	1					
	1					
	1					

Flippo, McCovey, and Stanford Partnership
Statement of Liquidation
January 1, 20x3

Explanation	Cash	Accounts Receivable	Land	Building (net)	Office Equipment (net)	Accounts Payable	Mortgage Payable	Flippo, Capital (33.3%)	McCovey, Capital (33.3%)	Stanford, Capital (33.3%)	Gain (or Loss) from Realization
Balance 1/1/x3											

1. Distribution calculated for income of $84,000

	Income of Partner		Income
	Gloria	Dennis	Distributed

2. Distribution calculated for income of $44,000

	Income of Partner		Income
	Gloria	Dennis	Distributed

3. | **Distribution calculated for $12,800 loss**

	Income (Loss) of Partner		Loss Distributed
	Gloria	Dennis	

a.	July	31			
b.	July	31			
c.	July	31			

Computation:

Maureen's interest	(	x	0.20)	
Bonus to the original partners				*

*Partners' capital ratios:

Partner	Capital Balance	Ratios	
Renee		/	180
Esther		/	
Jane		/	
		/	

Distribution of bonus to original partners:

Renee (		x	÷	180)	
Esther (		x	÷	)	
Jane (		x	÷	)	
Total bonus					

d.	July	31				

Computation:

Maureen's interest	(		x	0.40	)	
Bonus to Maureen						*

***Distribution of bonus from original partners:**

Renee (		x	÷	180)	
Esther (		x	÷	)	
Jane (		x	÷	)	
Total bonus					
Partners' capital ratios: See answer to part *c*.					

e.	July	31				
			Withdrawal of Renee from			
			the partnership*			

***Distribution of excess cash over Renee's capital balance between the
remaining partners:**

Esther (		x	÷	90)
Jane (		x	÷	)

f.	July	31				

1. Statement of liquidation prepared

Nguyen, Waters, and Leach Partnership
Statement of Liquidation
June 1–11, 20x3

Explanation	Cash	Other Assets	Accounts Payable	Nguyen, Capital (40%)	Waters, Capital (40%)	Leach, Capital (20%)	Gain (or Loss) from Realization
Balance 5/31/x3							
a. Sale of Other Assets							
b. Payment of Liabilities							
c. Distribution of Gain (or Loss) from Realization							
d. Distribution to Partners							

2.	Entries in journal form prepared								
a.	June	1							
b.		4							
c.		11							
			Distribution of the loss on assets to the partners						
			Nguyen:			x	0.40	=	
			Waters:			x		=	
			Leach:			x		=	
d.		11							
			Distribution of cash to the partners						
			Nguyen:						
				−			=		
			Waters:						
				−			=		
			Leach:						
				−			=		

1.

2.

Projected income before salaries

	20x1	20x2	20x3	20x4	20x5

3.

4.

Chapter 14, SE 1.

1.		5.	
2.		6.	
3.		7.	
4.			

Chapter 14, SE 2.

1.		4.	
2.		5.	
3.		6.	

Chapter 14, SE 3.

Start-up and Organization Costs	
Legal services, 3,000 shares of $1 par value common stock	
Incorporation fees	
Total start-up and organization costs	
Income Statement Effect	
Start-up and Organization Expense	
Balance Sheet Effect	
Retained Earnings	

Chapter 14, SE 4.

Lincoln Corporation			
Balance Sheet			
December 31, 20xx			
Stockholders' Equity			

Chapter 14, SE 5.

May	15				
		Declared a cash dividend of $0.10 per outstanding share			
		shares x	=		
June	1				
	15				

Chapter 14, SE 6.

	Preferred Stock Dividends		Common Stock Dividends		Total Dividends Allocated
	Amount	Per Share	Amount	Per Share	
20x1					
20x2					
20x1 dividends in arrears					
(x 0.08)					
20x2 dividends					
(x)					
(–)					
Totals					
20x3					
20x3 dividends					
(x 0.08)					
(–)					
Totals					

Chapter 14, SE 7.

1.

2.

Chapter 14, SE 8.

1.

		Issued 8,000 shares of $1 par value common stock for land; market value of common stock used to value transaction		
		shares at ___ = ___		

2.

Chapter 14, SE 9.

Oct.	1				
		Acquired 1,000 shares of company's common stock for $20,000			
		(x per share)			
	17				
		Sold 250 shares of treasury stock for			
		(x per share);			
		cost was (x			
		per share)			
	21				
		Sold 400 shares of treasury stock for			
		(x per share);			
		cost was (x			
		per share)			

Chapter 14, SE 10.

Oct.	28				

Chapter 14, SE 11.

June	6				

Chapter 14, E 1.

Dividends Yield =	
=	___ **=**
Price/Earnings (P/E) Ratio =	
=	___ **=** **times**

Chapter 14, E 2.

Hagor Corporation Balance Sheet December 31, 20xx Stockholders' Equity		

Chapter 14, E 3.

1.		4.		7.	
2.		5.		8.	
3.		6.		9.	

Chapter 14, E 4.

1. Journal entries prepared

20xx					
Mar.	1				
	1				

2. Stockholders' equity section of the balance sheet prepared

Prada Hospital Supply Corporation
Balance Sheet
March 1, 20xx
Stockholders' Equity

Contributed Capital		

Chapter 14, E 5.

June	5				
			Declared a $.50 cash dividend to common stockholders		
			shares x =		
	15				
	25				

Chapter 14, E 6.

Oct.	15				
			Declared a $.25 cash dividend to common stockholders		
			issued shares –		
			treasury shares = shares outstanding		
			shares x =		
Nov.	1				
	15				

	Preferred Stock Dividends		Common Stock Dividends		Total
	Amount	Per Share	Amount	Per Share	Dividends Allocated
20x1					
20x2					
20x1 dividends in arrears					
(x)					
20x2 dividends					
(−)					
Totals					
20x3					
20x2 dividends in arrears					
(−)					
20x3 dividends					
(x)					
(−)					
Totals					
20x4					
20x4 dividends					
(x)					
(−)					
Totals					

					Preferred Stock Dividends	Common Stock Dividends	Total
1.	20x1 dividends						
	20x2 dividends						
	20x3 dividends						
	(		x	0.06)			
	(		–	)			
2.	20x1 dividends						
	(		x	)			
	(		–	)			
	20x2 dividends						
	20x3 dividends						
	20x2 dividends in arrears						
	(		–	)			
	20x3						
	(		x	)			
	(		–	)			
	Totals						

Chapter 14, E 9.

1. Journal entry prepared—$25 par value

Aug.	1			

2. Journal entry prepared—$10 par value

Aug.	1			

3. Journal entry prepared—no par value

Aug.	1			

4. Journal entry prepared—$1 stated value

Aug.	1			

Chapter 14, E 10.

1.   Journal entry prepared—$10 par value

20xx					
July	1				

2.   Journal entry prepared—no par value

20xx					
July	1				

3.   Journal entry prepared—$4 stated value

20xx					
July	1				

Chapter 14, E 11.

May	**5**				
			Acquired 400 shares of the company's common stock for (shares x		
			per share)		
	17				
			Sold 150 shares of treasury stock for		
			(shares x per share); cost		
			was (shares x per		
			share)		
	21				
			Sold 100 shares of treasury stock for		
			(shares x per share), an		
			amount equal to cost		
	28				
			Sold 150 shares of treasury stock for		
			(shares x per share); cost		
			was (shares x per		
			share)		

June	1			
		Acquired 2,000 shares of the company's		
		common stock for (		
		shares x per share)		
	10			
		Sold 500 shares of treasury stock for		
		(shares x		
		per share); cost was		
		(shares x per share)		
	20			
		Sold 700 shares of treasury stock for		
		(shares x per		
		share); cost was (		
		shares x per share)		
	30			
		Retired 800 shares of treasury stock;		
		cost was (shares x		
		per share); originally issued at		
		(shares x		
		per share)		

Chapter 14, E 13.

Estimate of compensation expense on the option grant date recorded

20x3							
Jan.	1						
			Estimated cost of stock options granted				
			shares x (		–	)	
			=				

Alternative to recording the above entry

Exercise of option recorded

20x3							
Nov.	30						

1. | Journal entries prepared

Sept.	1				
			Issued shares of		
			par value common stock for		
			per share		
	1				
Oct.	2				
Nov.	30				
			Declared a $0.40 cash dividend		
			to common stockholders		
			shares x =		

2. | **Stockholders' equity section of the balance sheet prepared**

Sussex Corporation	
Balance Sheet	
November 30, 20xx	
Stockholders' Equity	
Contributed Capital	

Chapter 14, P 2.

1. Dividends calculated for cumulative preferred and common stock

	Cumulative Preferred Stock Dividends		Common Stock Dividends		Total Dividends Allocated
	Amount	Per Share	Amount	Per Share	
20x2					
20x3					
Dividends in arrears,					
20x2					
20x3 dividends					
Totals					
20x4					

2. Dividends calculated for noncumulative preferred and common stock

	Noncumulative Preferred Stock Dividends		Common Stock Dividends		Total Dividends Allocated
	Amount	Per Share	Amount	Per Share	
20x2					
20x3					
20x4					

3. The 20x3 and 20x4 dividends yield for common stock calculated

	20x3		20x4		
Dividends per Share		=		=	
Market Price per Share					

Chapter 14, P 3.

a.

Purchased   shares of common stock
for the treasury at   per share

b.

c.

Sold   shares of treasury stock for
; originally purchased for
per share
shares x   =

d.

e.

f.

1. **Transactions recorded**

Aug.	3					
		Issued		shares of	stated		
		value common stock for organization				
		services valued at				
	15					
	22					
Oct.	4					
	10					
	15					
		Declared preferred and common stock cash				
		dividends				
			x	+ 4 =		
			shares x	$0.10	=	
	25					
	31					

2. Stockholders' equity section of the balance sheet prepared

Kokaly Plastics Corporation		
Balance Sheet		
October 31, 20xx		
Stockholders' Equity		

Chapter 14, P 5.

1. Transactions recorded in T accounts

Cash			
1/19		3/22	
7/15		9/25	
8/1			
12/15			
Bal.			

Land			

Preferred Stock			

Building			

Paid-in Capital in Excess of Stated Value, Common			

Cash Dividends Payable			

Common Stock			

Retained Earnings			

Cash Dividends Declared			

Paid-in Capital, Treasury Stock			

Start-up and Organization Expense			

Treasury Stock, Common			

Chapter 14, P 5. (Continued)

2. **Stockholders' equity section of the balance sheet prepared**

Jones Corporation		
Balance Sheet		
December 31, 20xx		
Stockholders' Equity		

Chapter 14, P 6.						
1. Transactions recorded						
Mar.	**1**					
	2					
Apr.	**10**					
May	**31**					
			Declared a cash dividend of $.20 per share			
			(shares x =)			

2. Stockholders' equity section of balance sheet prepared

Carmel Corporation
Balance Sheet
May 31, 20xx
Stockholders' Equity

Chapter 14, P 7.

1. Dividends calculated for cumulative preferred and common stock

	Cumulative Preferred Stock Dividends		Common Stock Dividends		Total Dividends Allocated
	Amount	Per Share	Amount	Per Share	
20x1					

2. Dividends calculated for noncumulative preferred and common stock

	Noncumulative Preferred Stock Dividends		Common Stock Dividends		Total Dividends Allocated
	Amount	Per Share	Amount	Per Share	

3. The 20x3 and 20x4 dividends yield for common stock calculated

	20x3		20x4		
Dividends per Share		=		=	
Market Price per Share					

Chapter 14, P 8.

1. **Transactions recorded**

July	**1**				
		Issued	**shares of**	**stated**	
		value common stock at		**per share**	
	1				
	2				
	10				
Aug.	**2**				
	10				
		Declared preferred and common stock			
		cash dividends			
		x	x	÷ **12** =	
		shares x		=	
	12				
	22				

2. Stockholders' equity section of the balance sheet prepared

Vanowski, Inc.		
Balance Sheet		
August 31, 20xx		
Stockholders' Equity		

Chapter 14, SD 6.

1.   Schedule of alternatives prepared

Northeast Servotech Corporation Schedule of Financing Alternatives 20xx	Alternatives		
	A	B	C
Liabilities			
Total Liabilities			
Stockholders' Equity			
Total Stockholders' Equity			
Total Liabilities and Stockholders' Equity			
Debt to equity ratio			

Chapter 14, SD 6. (Continued)	

2. Cash requirements for the first year computed

Alternative A	
Interest on long-term debt	
(x 0.12)	
Tax savings (40%)	
Annual cash requirement, after tax	
Alternative B	
Dividends on preferred stock	
(x 0.08)	
Alternative C	
Dividends on common stock	
(shares x $1)	

3. Cash requirements in future years discussed

4.	Memorandum prepared

Memorandum

Date:	
To:	
From:	
Re:	

Chapter 14, FRA 1.

1. Stock issue recorded

1996					
Nov.	14				

2. Stockholders' equity section of the balance sheet prepared

Netscape Communications Corporation
Balance Sheet
November 14, 1996
Stockholders' Equity
(in thousands)

3. **Netscape's need to increase the authorized shares discussed**

4. **Underwriters' fee discussed**

Chapter 14, FRA 2.

(Answers, except per share amounts and percentages, are in millions)

Dividends per share:

$$\frac{}{} = \frac{}{} = \text{Swiss francs (SFr.)}$$

Dividends yield:

$$\frac{}{} = \frac{}{} =$$

Increase in retained earnings plus dividends = 1999 earnings

	−		+		=	

In U.S. dollars:

	÷		=		million

Return on equity:

$$\frac{}{} = \big(+ \big) \div$$

$$= \frac{}{} =$$

1.

2.

3.

4.

5.

Price/Earnings Ratio	=			
2000	=		=	**times**
1999	=		=	

Return on Equity	=			
2000	=	(	+	) ÷
	=			
1999	=	(	+	) ÷
	=			

Chapter 15, SE 1.

1.	
2.	
3.	
4.	
5.	
6.	
7.	
8.	

Chapter 15, SE 2.

<table>
<tr><td colspan="3" align="center">Griswold Company
Income Statement
For the Year Ended June 30, 20xx</td></tr>
<tr><td>Net Sales</td><td></td><td></td></tr>
<tr><td></td><td></td><td></td></tr>
<tr><td></td><td></td><td></td></tr>
<tr><td></td><td></td><td></td></tr>
<tr><td></td><td></td><td></td></tr>
<tr><td></td><td></td><td></td></tr>
<tr><td>Discontinued Operations</td><td></td><td></td></tr>
<tr><td>Loss from Operations of Discontinued Segment (net of taxes, $70,000)</td><td></td><td></td></tr>
<tr><td>Loss on Disposal of Segment (net of taxes, $16,000)</td><td></td><td></td></tr>
<tr><td>Net Loss</td><td></td><td></td></tr>
</table>

Chapter 15, SE 3.

1. Taxable income of _____
   _____ + [(_____ − _____) x _____] = _____

2. Taxable income of _____
   _____ + [(_____ − _____) x _____]
   = _____

Chapter 15, SE 4.

Weighted-average number of common shares computed:

20x1	_____ x _____ + _____ year _____	= _____
	(_____ + _____) x _____ + 12 year = _____
	Total shares
20x2	_____ x _____ + 12 year _____	= _____

Earnings per share computed:

	20x1	20x2
Net income		
Weighted-average common stock		
Earnings per share of common stock		

Chapter 15, SE 5.

		per share (		÷		shares)
1.						
2.						
3.						
4.						

Chapter 15, SE 6.

	Total Assets	Total Liabilities	Total Stockholders' Equity	
1.				
2.				
3.				
4.				
5.				

Chapter 15, SE 7.

	Retained Earnings (Note *x*)	
Note x:		

Feb.	**15**				
			Declaration of a stock dividend of 2,200 shares		
			(2% x 110,000 shares) on $10 par value		
			common stock, to be distributed on March 15,		
			at the market value of stock of		
			(shares x per share)		
Mar.	**1**				
	15				
	30				
			Declaration of a cash dividend		
			x shares =		

Chapter 15, SE 9.

After Stock Split

Symula International Stockholders' Equity August 10, 20xx	
Contributed Capital	
Retained Earnings	
Total Stockholders' Equity	

No entry is required, but a memorandum entry for informational purposes should be prepared.

Chapter 15, SE 10.

Preferred Stock Book Value per Share	=	(		x		) +		*
						shares		
	=			=		per share		
* (	shares	x		x		) =		
Common Stock Book Value per Share =					−			
					shares			
	=			=		per share		

Chapter 15, E 1.	
1. **Net income determined under FIFO**	
Net income under average-cost method	
Difference between FIFO and average-cost inventory	
(–)	
Net income under FIFO	

2. **Net income determined under LIFO**	
Net income under average-cost method	
Difference between average-cost and LIFO inventory	
(–)	
Net income under LIFO	

3.

4.

5.

Abbey Furniture Company		
Income Statement		
For the Year Ended June 30, 20xx		

Burda Corporation
Income Statement
For the Year Ended December 31, 20x1

Sales		
Earnings per Common Share:		

Chapter 15, E 4.

Situation A

| | | + [(| | − | |) × | 0.25 |] | = | |

Situation B

| | | + [(| | − | |) × | |] | = | |

Situation C

| | | + [(| | − | |) × | |] | = | |

Chapter 15, E 5.

1. Amount of taxes paid computed

	20x2	20x3

2. Entries in journal form prepared

20x2					
20x3					

Chapter 15, E 6.

1.   Weighted-average number of common shares computed

20x1		shares x	÷ 12	year	=	
		shares x	÷	year	=	
	Total weighted average shares					
20x2		+			=	

2.   Earnings per share computed

	20x1	20x2

Chapter 15, E 7.

Retained Earnings (Note *x*)	

Note x:

Farhad Corporation
Statement of Stockholders' Equity
For the Year Ended December 31, 20x3

	9%, $100 Par Value Cumulative Preferred Stock	$2 Par Value Common Stock	Paid-in Capital in Excess of Par Value, Common	Retained Earnings	Treasury Stock	Total
Balance, December 31, 20x2						
a.						
b.						
c.						
d.						
e.						
f.						
Balance, December 31, 20x3						

July	17					
			Declaration of a 3,000-share stock dividend (30,000 shares x .10) on $1 par value common stock, to be distributed on August 10, at the market value of stock of			
			(shares x per share)			
	31					
Aug.	10					
Sept.	1					
			Declaration of a cash dividend			
			shares x =			

Before Stock Split

Hao Company	
Stockholders' Equity	
May 15, 20xx	

After Stock Split

Hao Company	
Stockholders' Equity	
May 15, 20xx	

Chapter 15, E 11.

Before Stock Split

	Imhoff International Stockholders' Equity January 15, 20xx	

After Stock Split

	Imhoff International Stockholders' Equity January 15, 20xx	

Preferred Stock Book Value per Share	=	(		x		) +			*
					shares				

	=		=		per share

*(		shares	x		x	0.06	) =	

Common Stock Book Value per Share	=		–		
			shares		

	=		=		per share

1. **Alternative income statements prepared**

Zalme Company			
Alternative Income Statements			
For the Year Ended December 31, 20xx			
Income Statement Using FIFO			
and Straight-Line Methods			
Net Sales			
Cost of Goods Sold			
Purchases			
Less Ending Inventory			
units at			
units at			
Cost of Goods Sold			
Gross Margin			
Operating Expenses			
Salaries Expense			
Other Expenses			
Depreciation			
÷ years			
Total Operating Expenses			
Net Income			

Income Statement Using LIFO			
and Double-Declining-Balance Methods			
Net Sales			
Cost of Goods Sold			
Purchases			
Less Ending Inventory			
units at			
units at			
Cost of Goods Sold			
Gross Margin			
Operating Expenses			
Salaries Expense			
Other Expenses			
Depreciation			
X			
Total Operating Expenses			
Net Income			

2. Schedule prepared

Zalme Company Schedule of Differences in Net Income For the Year Ended December 31, 20xx		
Difference in net income		
Net income using FIFO and straight-line methods		
Net income using LIFO and double-declining-balance methods		
Difference in net income		
Differences resulting from alternative methods		
Cost of goods sold		
LIFO		
FIFO		
Depreciation		
Double-declining-balance method		
Straight-line method		
Difference in net income		

3. Inventory turnover computed and discussed

Inventory Turnover	FIFO Method			LIFO Method		
		=	times		=	times

4.   Return on assets computed and discussed

Return on Assets		FIFO/SL Methods					
	=						
			+		+		−
	=		=				
		LIFO/DDB Methods					
	=						
			+		+		−
	=		=				

Norris Weather Gear Corporation
Income Statement
For the Year Ended December 31, 20xx

Earnings per Common Share:

1. Income statement prepared

	Dasbol Corporation Income Statements For the Years Ended December 31, 20x3 and 20x2		
		20x3	20x2
Earnings per Common Share:			

2. **Restructuring plan assessed**

601

Chapter 15, P 4.

1. Transactions recorded in T accounts

Common Stock				Paid-in Capital in Excess of Par Value, Common				
		Bal.						
		4/5						
		Bal.						

Common Stock Distributable				Stock Dividends Declared				
				2/28		1		
				12/31		2		
		Bal.		*Bal.*				

Treasury Stock				Retained Earnings				
						Bal.		

Bal.				

| 1. | | shares | x | 0.10 | x | | = | |
| 2. | | shares | x | | x | | = | |

| Shares outstanding before split: | | + | | = | |
| Shares outstanding after split: | | x | | = | |

March 25 —

August 3 —

2. Stockholders' equity section of the balance sheet prepared

Pittman Corporation		
Stockholders' Equity		
December 31, 20x5		
Contributed Capital		

Chapter 15, P 5.

1. Transactions recorded

20x3							
Mar.	5						
			Declaration of a cash dividend				
				shares	x	=	
	20						
Apr.	6						
June	17						
			Declaration of a stock dividend of 50,000 shares (500,000 shares x .10) on $2 par value common stock, to be distributed on August 17, at the market value of the stock				
				shares	x	=	
Aug.	5						
	17						
Oct.	2	Memo:					
Dec.	27						
			Declaration of a cash dividend				
				shares	x	=	

2. **Stockholders' equity section of the balance sheet prepared**

Rigby Moving and Storage Company	
Stockholders' Equity	
December 31, 20x3	

Note x:

1. **Transactions recorded**

20x2					
Jan.	4				
	14				
	14				
Mar.	8	Memo:			
Apr.	20				
May	4				
July	15				
		Declared a cash dividend of $4 per share on 14,000 shares of preferred stock and $.40 per share on 118,000 shares of common stock			
		+	=		
	25				

20x2					
Aug.	**15**				
Nov.	**28**				
		Declared a 15 percent stock dividend on			
		118,000 shares of common stock; market			
		value was $20 per share; par value is $4			
		per share			
		shares x	=		
Dec.	**15**				

Chapter 15, P 6. (Continued)

T accounts for stockholders' equity

Preferred Stock			

Common Stock			

Common Stock Distributable			

Paid-in Capital in Excess of Par Value, Common			

Paid-in Capital, Treasury Stock			

Retained Earnings			
7/15/x2		*	
11/28/x2		*	

* **Cash dividends declared and stock dividends declared reduce retained earnings.**

Treasury Stock, Common			

2. | **Stockholders' equity section of the balance sheet prepared**

<table>
<tr><td colspan="3" align="center">**Toczycki Company**
Stockholders' Equity
December 31, 20x2</td></tr>
<tr><td></td><td></td><td></td></tr>
<tr><td></td><td></td><td></td></tr>
<tr><td></td><td></td><td></td></tr>
<tr><td></td><td></td><td></td></tr>
<tr><td></td><td></td><td></td></tr>
<tr><td></td><td></td><td></td></tr>
<tr><td></td><td></td><td></td></tr>
<tr><td></td><td></td><td></td></tr>
<tr><td></td><td></td><td></td></tr>
<tr><td></td><td></td><td></td></tr>
<tr><td></td><td></td><td></td></tr>
<tr><td></td><td></td><td></td></tr>
<tr><td></td><td></td><td></td></tr>
<tr><td></td><td></td><td></td></tr>
<tr><td></td><td></td><td></td></tr>
<tr><td></td><td></td><td></td></tr>
<tr><td></td><td></td><td></td></tr>
</table>

Note *x* :

3. | **Book value per share computed**

December 31, 20x1

Common Stock:

| | | ÷ | | shares | = | | per share |

December 31, 20x2

Preferred Stock:

Common Stock:

| (| | − | |) ÷ (| | shares | + | | shares) |
| = | | ÷ | | shares | = | | per share |

Sim Corporation
Income Statement
For the Year Ended December 31, 20x1

Earnings per Common Share:

Chapter 15, P 8.

1. Transactions recorded in T accounts

Common Stock						Common Stock Distributable		
			Bal.					
			5/1					
			Bal.					

Paid-in Capital in Excess of Par Value, Common						Retained Earnings		

Stock Dividends Declared				
3/25			1	
12/15			2	
Bal.				

1.		X		X		=	
2.		X		X		=	

Shares outstanding before split:		+		=	
Shares outstanding after split:		X		=	

April 20 —

September 10 —

2. **Stockholders' equity section of the balance sheet prepared**

<table>
<tr><td colspan="2" align="center">**Waterbury Linen Mills, Inc.**
Stockholders' Equity
December 31, 20x3</td></tr>
<tr><td></td><td></td></tr>
<tr><td></td><td></td></tr>
<tr><td></td><td></td></tr>
<tr><td></td><td></td></tr>
<tr><td></td><td></td></tr>
<tr><td></td><td></td></tr>
<tr><td></td><td></td></tr>
<tr><td></td><td></td></tr>
</table>

Chapter 15, P 9.

1. Transactions recorded

20x1					
Dec.	17				
20x2					
Jan.	1				
	20				
Apr.	14				
May	1				
	15				
June	17	Memo:			
Sept.	15				

Chapter 15, P 9. (Continued)

2. **Stockholders' equity section of the balance sheet prepared**

O'Connor Woolen Company Stockholders' Equity September 30, 20x2	

Note x:

Chapter 15, SD 3.

1. Earnings per share computed

	20x3	20x2	20x1

2. Bonuses discussed

1. **Stockholders' equity section prepared (in thousands of dollars)**

	Common Stock			

	Common Stock Distributable			

	Paid-in Capital in Excess of Par Value, Common			

	Retained Earnings			

	Treasury Stock, Common		

	Common Stock Outstanding (in thousands of shares)			

Metzger Steel Corporation Stockholders' Equity December 31, 20x2	

2. **Arnold Metzger's position analyzed and discussed**

Memorandum
Date:
To:
From:
Re:

Arnold Metzger's shares:

Original holding, December 31, 20x1		shares
Stock split		
10 percent stock dividend (when issued)		
Ending holding, December 31, 20x2		

Book value computations, December 31, 20x1

Stockholders' Equity	÷	Common Stock Outstanding	=	Book Value per Share
	÷	shares	=	per share

Shares Owned	x	Book Value per Share	=	Metzger's Book Value
	x		=	

Shares Owned	÷	Common Stock Outstanding	=	Metzger's Percentage Ownership
	÷		=	

Book value computations, December 31, 20x2 (after stock dividend)

Stockholders' Equity	÷	Common Stock Outstanding	=	Book Value per Share
	÷	shares	=	

Shares Owned	x	Book Value per Share	=	Metzger's Book Value
	x		=	

Shares Owned	÷	Common Stock Outstanding	=	Metzger's Percentage Ownership
	÷		=	

	Redeemed and retired		shares		
	of preferred stock at par value of				
	Purchased	shares of	par		
	value common stock at an average price of				
	per share (	÷			
	) by employees under stock option				
	plan				
	Purchased	shares of common			
	stock at an average price of		per		
	share (	÷	)		
	for the treasury				

	Converted convertible debentures into		
	shares of common stock at an		
	exchange rate of	per share		
	(÷)		
	Issued shares of common		
	stock for cash at per share		
	(÷)		
	Exchanged common shares for		
	shares in Electrix Company as an investment;		
	the value of the transaction is per		
	share (÷)		

Chapter 15, FRA 2.

1. Income taxes expense computed (in millions) and entry in journal form to record income taxes prepared

Current income tax provision	
Deferred income tax provision	
Income taxes expense on the income statement	

2. Deferred income taxes as a liability discussed

Chapter 16, SE 1.

1.	
2.	
3.	
4.	
5.	

Chapter 16, SE 2.

20x1								
Apr.	1							
			Issued 8.5 percent, five-year bonds at 98					
				x	0.98	=		
Oct.	1							
			Paid semiannual interest and amortized discount					
			÷ (		years x	) =		
				x	0.085	x	/ 12	
			=					
20x2								
Apr.	1							
			Paid semiannual interest and amortized discount					
			÷ (		years x	) =		
				x		x	/	
			=					

Chapter 16, SE 3.

20xx						
Mar.	1					
Aug.	31					
			To record accrued semiannual interest and amortized premium on 9.5 percent, 20-year bonds			
			(x 0.095 x / 12)			
			− (x x /)			
			= − =			
Sept.	1					

Chapter 16, SE 4.

Choice A

Present value of 40 periodic payments at 6 percent (from Table 4*)				
		x	15.046	
Present value of a single payment at the end of 40 periods at 6 percent (from Table 3*)				
		x		
Total present value of Choice A				

Choice B

Present value of 30 periodic payments at 6 percent (from Table 4*)				
		x		
Present value of a single payment at the end of 30 periods at 6 percent (from Table 3*)				
		x		
Total present value of Choice B				
Total present value of both bonds				

*From the appendix on future value and present value tables.

Chapter 16, SE 5.

a.	Sept.	1			
			Sold bonds at 100 plus three months' accrued interest		
			x 0.08 x ⋅ / 12 =		
b.	June	1			

Chapter 16, SE 6.

1. Journal entries prepared

20xx					
Sept.	1				
			Sold $200,000 of 9 percent, ten-year bonds at face value plus accrued interest		
			x x / =		
Nov.	1				
			Made semiannual interest payment		
			x x / =		

Bond interest expense calculated

Chapter 16, SE 7.

20x1											
Oct.	1										
Dec.	31										
			To record accrued bond interest expense and amortize bond discount								
			(		x	0.10	x		/ 12)		
			− (		x		x	/	)		
			=		−		=				
20x2											
Apr.	1										
			Made semiannual interest payment and amortized bond discount								
					x		x	/	=		

Chapter 16, SE 8.

Dec.	1				
		Retired 8 percent bonds at call price of 104			
		x	1.04	=	
		_____ x	=		

Chapter 16, SE 9.

20x2					
Mar.	1				
		Converted $600,000 of 6 percent bonds into common stock at the rate of 20 shares for each $1,000 bond			
		x	shares	=	shares
		shares x	=		
		_____ x	=		
		− (	+	)	
		=			

Chapter 16, SE 10.

Month	Monthly Payment	Interest for 1 Month at .6667%* on Unpaid Balance	Reduction in Debt	Unpaid Balance at End of Period	
0					
1					
2					
3					

*	8%	÷		=	

Chapter 16, E 1.

Interest Coverage Ratio	=	+

20x1	=	+

	=	times

20x2	=	+

	=	times

Chapter 16, E 2.

20x1											
Feb.	1										
Aug.	1										
			Paid semiannual interest and amortized the premium								
			÷ (		years	x	) =				
			x (			÷	) =				
			−			=					
20x2											
Feb.	1										
			Paid semiannual interest and amortized the premium								
			÷ (		years	x	) =				
			x (			÷	) =				
			−			=					

Chapter 16, E 3.

20x1											
Mar.	1										
Sept.	1										
			Paid semiannual interest and amortized the discount								
			÷ (		years	x	) =				
			(			÷	) =				
			+			=					
20x2											
Mar.	1										
			Paid semiannual interest and amortized the discount								
			÷ (		years	x	) =				
			(			÷	) =				
			+			=					

Chapter 16, E 4.

20xx												
Apr.	1											
Sept.	30											
			Accrued semiannual interest and amortized the premium on 9.5 percent, 20-year bonds									
			(		x	0.095	x		/ 12	)	–	
			(		x		x		/	)	=	
				–			=					
Oct.	1											

20x1														
Mar.	1													
Sept.	1													
			Paid semiannual interest and amortized the discount on 10 percent, five-year bonds											
			(		x	0.11	x		/12	)	−			
			(		x		x		/		)	=		
				−			=							
20x2														
Feb.	28													
			To record accrued semiannual interest and amortized discount on 10 percent, five-year bonds											
			(		x		x		/		)	−		
			(		x		x		/		)	=		
				−			=							
Mar.	1													
			Made semiannual interest payment											

Chapter 16, E 6.

Choice A		

Choice B		

Chapter 16, E 7.

a.	Present value of 20 periodic payments at 5 percent				
	(from Table 4*):	$48,000	x		
	Present value of a single payment at the end of 20 periods				
	at 5 percent				
	(from Table 3*):			x	
	Issue price (total present value) of bond issue				
b.	Present value of 20 periodic payments at 3 percent				
	(from Table 4*):			x	
	Present value of a single payment at the end of 20 periods				
	at 3 percent				
	(from Table 3*):			x	
	Issue price (total present value) of bond issue				
c.	Present value of 20 periodic payments at 4 percent				
	(from Table 4*):			x	
	Present value of a single payment at the end of 20 periods				
	at 4 percent				
	(from Table 3*):			x	
	Issue price (total present value) of bond issue				
d.	Present value of 40 periodic payments at 6 percent				
	(from Table 4*):			x	
	Present value of a single payment at the end of 40 periods				
	at 6 percent				
	(from Table 3*):			x	
	Issue price (total present value) of bond issue				
e.	Present value of 40 periodic payments at 3 percent				
	(from Table 4*):			x	
	Present value of a single payment at the end of 40 periods				
	at 3 percent				
	(from Table 3*):			x	
	Issue price (total present value) of bond issue				

*From the appendix on future value and present value tables.

Chapter 16, E 8.

Face value of 30-year, 10 percent zero coupon bonds, compounded annually:				
Present value of a single payment at the end of 30 periods at 10 percent (from Table 3*):				
Face value x		=	$100,000,000	
Face value =	$100,000,000	÷		
Face value =			or about	

Face value of 50-year, 10 percent zero coupon bonds, compounded annually:
Present value of a single payment at the end of 50 periods at 10 percent (from Table 3*):

Face value of 30-year, 8 percent zero coupon bonds, compounded annually:
Present value of a single payment at the end of 30 periods at 8 percent (from Table 3*):

Face value of 50-year, 8 percent zero coupon bonds, compounded annually:
Present value of a single payment at the end of 50 periods at 8 percent (from Table 3*):

*From the appendix on future value and present value tables.

2002													
July	1												
			Paid semiannual interest and amortized										
			the bond discount										
			(		x	0.10	x		/	12	)	–	
			(		x		x		/		)	=	
				–				=					
Dec.	31												
			To record accrued bond interest										
			expense and amortized bond discount										
			(		x		x		/		)	–	
			(		x		x		/		)	=	
				–				=					
2003													
Jan.	1												

a.	Sept.	1								
			Sold bonds at 100 plus three							
			months' accrued interest							
					x		x		/ 12	
				=						
b.	June	1								

Chapter 16, E 11.

1.   Journal entries prepared

20xx						
Sept.	1					
			Sold $400,000 of 12 percent, ten-year bonds at face value			
			x	0.12	x	/12
		=				
Nov.	1					
			Made semiannual interest payment			
			x		x	/

2.   Bond interest expense calculated

The bond interest expense for the year ended December 31, 20xx, is $16,000:

months (September–December) x   =

or

(–   ) + November (   )

+ December (   )   =

Chapter 16, E 12.

20x1						
Oct.	1					
Dec.	31					
			To record accrued bond interest expense and amortized bond discount			
			x	0.10	x	/12
		=				
			x		x	/
		=				
			–		=	
20x2						
Apr.	1					
			Made semiannual interest payment and amortized the bond discount			
			x		x	/
		=				

Chapter 16, E 13.			
1.	**Current market value of the bonds calculated**		

Present value of 20 periodic payments at 8 percent (16% ÷ 2)		
(from Table 4*):	X	
Present value of a single payment at the end of 20 periods		
with interest compounded semiannually at 8 percent (16% ÷ 2)		
(from Table 3*):	X	
Issue price (total present value) of bond issue		
***From the appendix on future value and present value tables.**		

2.	**Retirement of the bonds recorded**	

Chapter 16, E 14.

Sept.	1								
			Retired 8 percent bonds at call price						
			of 104						
				x	1.04	=			
			_____	x		=			

Chapter 16, E 15.

20x8									
July	1								
			Converted $300,000 of 6 percent bonds						
			into common stock at the rate of 40						
			shares for each $1,000 bond						
				x	shares	=	shares		
				shares	x		=		
			_____	x		=			

Chapter 16, E 16.

1. Monthly payment schedule prepared

Month	Monthly Payment	Interest for 1 Month at 1% on Unpaid Balance	Reduction in Debt	Unpaid Balance at End of Period
0				
1				
2				
3				

2. Journal entries prepared

Month 0				
Month 1				
Month 2				

Chapter 16, E 17.

1. Present value calculated

Periodic Payment x Factor (Table 4 in the appendix on future value and present value tables: 15%, 12 periods) = Present Value of Lease			
	X		=	

2. Journal entry prepared to record the lease agreement

3. Journal entry prepared to record depreciation for the first year

	To record depreciation on leased equipment for first year		
	÷	years		

4. Journal entries prepared to record lease payments

Year 1			
	Made lease payment for first year		
	X	=		
Year 2			
	Made lease payment for second year		
	(	−	) X	
	=		

Chapter 16, E 18.

20x1						
Dec.	**31**					
20x2						
Dec.	**31**					
			Made first installment payment on note			
			x	**0.12**	=	
20x3						
Dec.	**31**					
			Made second installment payment on note			
			x		=	

If the interest rate went up to 13 percent in the second year, the entry would be as follows:

20x3						
Dec.	**31**					
			Made second installment payment on note			
			x		=	

Chapter 16, E 19.

Using Table 4 from the appendix on future value and present value tables, the equal payment is calculated as follows:

Periodic Payment x Factor (Table 4 in the appendix on future value and present value tables: 12%, 4 years) = Present Value

Periodic Payment	x	3.037	=			
	Periodic Payment		=		÷	=

Payment schedule on $40,000, 12 percent installment note:

Payment Date	A Unpaid Principal at Beginning of Period	B Equal Annual Payment	C Interest for 1 Year at 12% on Unpaid Principal* (12% x A)	D Reduction in Principal (B − C)	E Unpaid Principal at End of Period (A − D)
					$40,000
20x2					
20x3					
20x4					
20x5					

* Rounded to the nearest dollar.

Entries for the first two payments:

20x2 Dec. 31				
20x3 Dec. 31				

1.   Journal entries prepared for bonds issued at more than face value

June	**1**				
Nov.	**30**				
			Paid semiannual interest and amortized the premium on 10.5 percent, 20-year bonds		
			÷ (20 x)		
			=		
			x 0.105 x / 12		
			=		
			− =		
Dec.	**31**				
			To record accrual of one month's interest expense and amortization of one month's bond premium on 10.5 percent, 20-year bonds		
			÷ x / 12		
			=		
			x x /		
			=		
			− =		

2.	Journal entries prepared for bonds issued at less than face value				

June	1				
Nov.	30				
			Paid semiannual interest and amortized the discount on 10.5 percent, 20-year bonds		
			÷ (x 2)		
			=		
			x 0.105 x / 12		
			=		
			+ =		
Dec.	31				
			To record accrual of one month's interest expense and amortization of one month's bond discount on 10.5 percent, 20-year bonds		
			÷ x / 12		
			=		
			x x /		
			=		
			+ =		

3. **Journal entries prepared for bonds issued at face value**

Aug.	1					
			Sold 10.5 percent, 20-year bonds			
			at face value plus two months'			
			accrued interest			
			x	0.105	x	/ 12
		=				
Nov.	30					
			Paid semiannual interest on 10.5			
			percent, 20-year bonds			
			x		x	/
		=				
Dec.	31					
			To record accrual of one month's			
			interest expense on 10.5 percent,			
			20-year bonds			
			x		x	/
		=				

1. Journal entries prepared for bonds issued at more than face value

Mar.	1											
Sept.	1											
			Paid semiannual interest and amortized the premium on 9.5 percent, 25-year bonds									
			(		x	0.095	x		/	12	)	−
			(		x		x		/		)	=
				−				=				
Nov.	30											
			To record accrual of three months' interest and amortization of the premium on 9.5 percent, 25-year bonds									
			(		x		x		/		)	−
			(		x		x		/		)	=
				−				=				

2. Journal entries prepared for bonds issued at less than face value

Mar.	1										
Sept.	1										
		Paid semiannual interest and amortized the discount on 9.5 percent, 25-year bonds									
		(		x	0.098	x		/ 12	) −		
		(		x		x		/	) =		
			−			=					
Nov.	30										
		To record accrual of three months' interest and amortization of the discount on 9.5 percent, 25-year bonds									
		(		x		x		/	) −		
		(		x		x		/	) =		
			−			=					

3. **Journal entries prepared for bonds issued at face value**

June	1									
			Sold 9.5 percent, 25-year bonds at							
			face value plus three months'							
			accrued interest							
				x	0.095	x		/ 12		
		=								
Sept.	1									
			Paid semiannual interest on 9.5							
			percent, 25-year bonds							
				x		x		/		
		=								
Nov.	30									
			To record accrual of three months'							
			interest on 9.5 percent, 25-year bonds							
				x		x		/		
		=								

20x2												
Jan.	1											
Mar.	1											
June	30											
			Paid semiannual interest on 9.9 percent, ten-year bonds and amortized the premium									
			(		x	x	/	)	−			
			(		x	x	/	)	=			
				−		=						
Sept.	1											
			Paid semiannual interest on 9.2 percent, ten-year bonds and amortized the discount									
			(		x	x	/	)	−			
			(		x	x	/	)	=			
				−		=						

20x2												
Dec.	31											
			Paid semiannual interest on 9.9 percent,									
			ten-year bonds and amortized the									
			premium									
			(		x		x	/		)	–	
			(		x		x	/		)	=	
				–			=					
	31											
			To record accrual of four months'									
			interest and amortization of the									
			discount on 9.2 percent, ten-year bonds									
			(		x		x	/		)	–	
			(		x		x	/		)	=	
				–			=					
20x3												
Mar.	1											
			Paid semiannual interest on 9.2									
			percent, ten-year bonds and amortized									
			the discount for the remainder of the									
			interest period									
			(		x		x	/		)	–	
			(		x		x	/		)	=	
				–			=					
					x		x	/ 2				
			=									

1. Bond interest and discount amortization table prepared

Semi-annual Interest Period	A Carrying Value at Beginning of Period	B Semiannual Interest Expense at 5% to Be Recorded (5% × A)	C Semiannual Interest to Be Paid to Bondholders (4-1/2% × $60,000,000)	D Amortization of Discount (B − C)	E Unamortized Bond Discount at End of Period (E − D)	F Carrying Value at End of Period (A + D)
0						
1						
2						
3						
4						
5						
6						
7						
8						
9						
10						
11						
12						

2. Calculate loss on early retirement of one-half of bonds payable on July 1, 20x4

Call price	× 1.05 =	
Carrying value	× 50% =	
Loss on early retirement		

20x3							
Nov.	1						
			Issued 12 percent bonds at face				
			value plus accrued interest				
				x	0.12	x	/ 12
		=					
20x4							
Jan.	31						
			Made semiannual interest payment				
			on 12 percent bonds				
				x		x	/
		=					
June	30						
			Recorded year-end accrual of				
			interest on 12 percent bonds				
				x		x	/
		=					
July	1						

20x4									
July	31								
Dec.	31								
			Made semiannual interest payment on 10 percent bonds and amortized the bond premium						
				x	0.10	x	/	12	=
				x		x	/		=
			Amortization						
20x5									
Jan.	31								
Feb.	28								
			Recorded accrual of interest expense for month prior to call						
				x		x	/		=
	28								
			Called 12 percent bonds at 104						
			(		x	1.04	)	+	
			=						

20x5										
June	30									
			Made semiannual interest payment on 10 percent bonds and amortized the bond premium							
				x	0.10	x	/	12	=	
				x		x	/		=	
			Amortization							
July	1									
			Converted 10 percent bonds into $10 par value common stock							
				x		shares	=		shares	
				shares	x		=			
				−	(		+		)	
			=							

Chapter 16, P 6.

1. Journal entries prepared for bonds issued at more than face value

Mar.	1										
Sept.	1										
			Paid semiannual interest and amortized the premium on 9.5 percent, 25-year bonds								
				÷ (		x	2	)	=		
					x	0.095	x	/		=	
				−				=			
Nov.	30										
			To record accrual of three months' interest and amortization of the premium on 9.5 percent, 25-year bonds								
				÷ (		x		/ 12	)	=	
					x		x	/		=	
				−				=			

2. Journal entries prepared for bonds issued at less than face value

Mar.	1										
Sept.	1										
			Paid semiannual interest and amortized the discount on 9.5 percent, 25-year bonds								
				÷ (		x	2	)	=		
					x		x	/		=	
				+				=			
Nov.	30										
			To record accrual of three months' interest and amortization of the discount on 9.5 percent, 25-year bonds								
				÷ (		x		/ 12	)	=	
					x		x	/		=	
				+				=			

3.   Journal entries prepared for bonds issued at face value

June	1							
			Sold 9.5 percent, 25-year bonds at face					
			value plus three months' accrued interest					
				x	0.095	x	/ 12 =	
Sept.	1							
			Paid semiannual interest on 9.5 percent,					
			25-year bonds					
				x		x	/ =	
Nov.	30							
			To record accrual of three months' interest					
			on 9.5 percent, 25-year bonds					
				x		x	/ =	

1. Journal entries prepared for bonds issued at more than face value

June	1			
Nov.	30			
		Paid semiannual interest and amortized the premium on 10.5 percent, 20-year bonds		
		(x 0.105 x 6 / 12) −		
		(x x /) =		
		− =		
Dec.	31			
		To record accrual of one month's interest expense on 10.5 percent, 20-year bonds		
		(x x / 12) −		
		(x x /) =		
		− =		

2. Journal entries prepared for bonds issued at less than face value

June	1			
Nov.	30			
		Paid semiannual interest and amortized the discount on 10.5 percent, 20-year bonds		
		(x x /) −		
		(x x /) =		
		− =		
Dec.	31			
		To record accrual of one month's interest expense on 10.5 percent, 20-year bonds		
		(x x /) −		
		(x x /) =		
		− =		

3. **Journal entries prepared for bonds issued at face value**

Aug.	1									
			Sold 10.5 percent, 20-year bonds at face							
			value plus 2 months' accrued interest							
				x	0.105	x		/	12 =	
Nov.	30									
			Paid semiannual interest on 10.5 percent,							
			20-year bonds							
				x		x		/	12 =	
Dec.	31									
			To record accrual of one month's interest							
			expense on 10.5 percent, 20-year bonds							
				x		x		/	=	

Chapter 16, P 8.

20x1														
Jan.	**1**													
Apr.	**1**													
June	**30**													
			Paid semiannual interest on 9.2 percent, ten-year bonds and amortized the discount											
			(		x		x	/12	)	–				
			(		x		x	/	)	=				
			–		=									
Sept.	**30**													
			Paid semiannual interest on 9.8 percent, ten-year bonds and amortized the premium											
			(		x		x	/12	)	–				
			(		x		x	/	)	=				
			–		=									
Dec.	**31**													
			Paid semiannual interest on 9.2 percent, ten-year bonds and amortized the discount											
			(		x		x	/12	)	–				
			(		x		x	/	)	=				
			–		=									

20x1												
Dec.	31											
			To record accrual of three months' interest and amortization of the premium on 9.8 percent, ten-year bonds								
			(	x	0.098	x	3	/	12	) –		
			(	x		x		/		) =		
			–			=						
20x2												
Mar.	31											

2006 Bond Issue

Present value of eight periodic payments at 4.0 percent (from Table 4*)

$4,500,000	x		=	

Present value of a single payment at the end of eight periods at 4.0 percent (from Table 3*)

	x		=	

Market value (total present value) of bond issue

2016 Bond Issue

Present value of 28 periodic payments at 4.0 percent (from Table 4*)

	x		=	

Present value of a single payment at the end of 28 periods at 4.0 percent (from Table 3*)

	x		=	

Market value (total present value) of bond issue

*Tables appear in appendix on future value and present value tables.

Interest Coverage Ratio	=	

(in millions of yen)

NEC		Sanyo	
1998	1997	1998	1997
+	+	+	+
times	times	times	times

1.

2.

Interest coverage ratios for the two most recent periods are:

Interest Coverage Ratio	=	

1999:	=	+
	=	times

2000:	=	+
	=	times

3.

4.

Chapter 17, SE 1.

1.		4.	
2.		5.	
3.		6.	

Chapter 17, SE 2.

Cash Flow Yield	=				
	=		=	times	
Cash Flows to Sales	=				
	=		=		
Cash Flows to Assets	=				
	=	(	+	) ÷	=
Free Cash Flow	=				
	=		−	−	+
	=				

Chapter 17, SE 3.

Chapter 17, SE 4.

Specialty Products Corporation		
Schedule of Cash Flows from Operating Activities		
For the Year Ended December 31, 20x1		

Chapter 17, SE 5.

Ayzarian Corporation		
Schedule of Cash Flows from Operating Activities		
For the Year Ended December 31, 20x1		

Chapter 17, SE 6.

Schedule of Noncash Investing and Financing Transactions

Chapter 17, SE 7.

Chapter 17, SE 8.

1.	5.
2.	6.
3.	7.
4.	8.

Chapter 17, SE 9.

Cash Receipts from Sales	=	Sales	+	Decrease in Accounts Receivable	(	–	)
	=		+				

Cash Payments for Purchases	=	Cost of Goods Sold	+	Increase in Inventory	(	–	)	+	Decrease in Accounts Payable	(	–	)
	=		+					+				
	=		+					+				

Chapter 17, SE 10.

Cash Payments for Operating Expenses	=	Operating Expenses	–	Decrease in Prepaid Expenses	+	Decrease in Accrued Liabilities	–	Depreciation Expense
	=		– (		) + (		) –	
	=		–		+		–	
	=							

Cash Payments for Income Taxes	=	Income Taxes Expense	+	Decrease in Income Taxes Payable
	=		+ (	)
	=		+	–

Chapter 17, E 1.

1.	6.	11.	
2.	7.	12.	
3.	8.	13.	
4.	9.		
5.	10.		

Chapter 17, E 2.

Cash Flow Yield	=				
	=		=	times	
Cash Flows to Sales	=				
	=		=		
Cash Flows to Assets	=				
	=	(	+	) ÷ 2	=
Free Cash Flow	=				
	=	−	−		
	=				

Green Fields Chem Company
Schedule of Cash Flows from Operating Activities
For the Year Ended December 31, 20x2

Chapter 17, E 4.

Boulevard Corporation
Schedule of Cash Flows from Operating Activities
For the Year Ended December 31, 20x1

Chapter 17, E 5.

Norris Corporation Schedule of Cash Flows from Operating Activities For the Year Ended June 30, 20xx		

Chapter 17, E 6.

Cash Flows from Investing Activities		
Purchase of Investments		(a)
Sale of Investments		(b)
a.		
b.		
The net cash flow from the sale is computed as follows:		

Chapter 17, E 7.

Cash Flows from Investing Activities

Purchase of Plant Assets		(a)
Sale of Plant Assets		(b)

a.

b.

The cash inflow from the disposal was:

Chapter 17, E 8.

Cash Flows from Financing Activities

Schedule of Noncash Investing and Financing Transactions

Tham Corporation
Statement of Cash Flows
For the Year Ended June 30, 20x2

Cash Flows from Investing Activities		

Schedule of Noncash Investing and Financing Transactions

Tham Corporation
Work Sheet for Statement of Cash Flows
For the Year Ended June 30, 20x2

Description	Account Balances 20x1	Analysis of Transactions		Account Balances 20x2
		Debit	Credit	
Debits				
Cash		(x)		
Credits				

Chapter 17, E 11.

a.	**Cash Receipts** **from Sales**	=	**Cash** **Sales**	+		+				
		=		+		+				
		=								
b.	**Cash Payments** **for Purchases**	=	**Cost of Goods** **Sold**	+		+				
		=		+		+				
		=								
c.	**Cash Payments** **for Operating** **Expenses**	=	**Operating** **Expenses**	−		−		−		
		=		−		−		−		
		=								
d.	**Cash Payments** **for Income Taxes**	=	**Income Taxes** **Expense**	+						
		=		+						
		=								

Vasquez Corporation							
Schedule of Cash Flows from Operating Activities							
For the Year Ended June 30, 20xx							
Cash Flows from Operating Activities							
Cash Receipts from Sales							**(a)**
Cash Payments for							
Purchases						**(b)**	
Operating Expenses						**(c)**	
Income Taxes						**(d)**	
Net Cash Flows from Operating Activities							
a.	**Cash Receipts**	=	**Sales**	–			
	from Sales	=		–			
		=					
b.	**Cash Payments**	=	**Cost of**	+		–	
	for Purchases		**Sold**				
		=		+		–	
		=					
c.	**Cash Payments**	=	**Operating**	–		–	–
	for Operating		**Expenses**				
	Expenses						
		=		–		–	–
		=					
d.	**Cash Payments**	=	**Income Taxes**	+			
	for Income Taxes		**Expense**				
		=		+			
		=					

| Transaction | Cash Flow Classification | | | | Effect on Cash | | |
	Operating Activity	Investing Activity	Financing Activity	Noncash Transaction	Increase	Decrease	No Effect
1. Incurred a net loss.							
2. Declared and issued a stock dividend.							
3. Paid a cash dividend.							
4. Collected accounts receivable.							
5. Purchased inventory with cash.							
6. Retired long-term debt with cash.							
7. Sold available-for-sale securities at a loss.							
8. Issued stock for equipment.							
9. Purchased a one-year insurance policy with cash.							
10. Purchased treasury stock with cash.							
11. Retired a fully depreciated truck (no gain or loss).							
12. Paid interest on note.							
13. Received cash dividend on investment.							
14. Sold treasury stock.							
15. Paid income taxes.							
16. Transferred cash to money market account.							
17. Purchased land and building with a mortgage.							

677

1. Statement of cash flows prepared

Sharma Fabrics, Inc.
Statement of Cash Flows
For the Year Ended December 31, 20x3

Schedule of Noncash Investing and Financing Transactions

Chapter 17, P 2. (Continued)

2. Causes of increase in cash identified

3. Computation and assessment of cash flow yield and free cash flow

Cash Flow Yield	=			
	=		=	**times**
Free Cash Flow	=			
	=	−	−	+
	=			

1. **Statement of cash flows prepared**

Karidis Ceramics, Inc.
Statement of Cash Flows
For the Year Ended December 31, 20x3

Schedule of Noncash Investing and Financing Transactions

2. Causes of decrease in cash identified

3. Computation and assessment of cash flow yield and free cash flow

Cash Flow Yield	=		
	=		=
Free Cash Flow	=		
	=	−	−
	=		

1. Work sheet prepared

Karidis Ceramics, Inc.
Work Sheet for Statement of Cash Flows
For the Year Ended December 31, 20x3

Description	Account Balances 12/31/x2	Analysis of Transactions		Account Balances 12/31/x3
		Debit	Credit	
Debits				
Cash			(x)	
Credits				

Description	Account Balances 12/31/x2	Analysis of Transactions		Account Balances 12/31/x3
		Debit	Credit	
Cash Flows from Operating Activities				
Net Income		(a)		
Cash Flows from Investing Activities				
Cash Flows from Financing Activities				
Net Decrease in Cash				

2. | Same as solutions to required 1, 2, and 3 in P 3.

Tanucci Clothing Store
Schedule of Cash Flows from Operating Activities
For the Year Ended June 30, 20xx

Cash Flows from Operating Activities						
Cash Receipts from Sales						(a)
Cash Payments for						
Purchases					(b)	
Operating Expenses					(c)	
Income Taxes					(d)	
Net Cash Flows from Operating Activities						

a.	Cash Receipts	=	Sales	−			
	from Sales	=		−			
		=					

b.	Cash Payments	=	Cost of Goods	+		−	
	for Purchases		Sold				
		=		+		−	
		=					

c.	Cash Payments	=	Operating	+		+		−	
	for Operating		Expenses						
	Expenses								
		=		+		+		− (	+
									)
		=							

d.	Cash Payments	=	Income Taxes	+	
	for Income Taxes				
		=		+	
		=			

1. Statement of cash flows prepared

O'Brien Corporation
Statement of Cash Flows
For the Year Ended December 31, 20x2

Schedule of Noncash Investing and Financing Transactions

Chapter 17, P 6. (Continued)

2. **Causes of increase in cash identified**

3. **Computation and assessment of cash flow yield and free cash flow**

Cash Flow Yield	=		

20x2:	=		=		times

Free Cash Flow	=	

20x2:	=		−		−		+	
	=							

Chapter 17, P 7.

Transaction	Cash Flow Classification				Effect on Cash		
	Operating Activity	Investing Activity	Financing Activity	Noncash Transaction	Increase	Decrease	No Effect
1. Earned a net income.							
2. Declared and paid cash dividend.							
3. Issued stock for cash.							
4. Retired long-term debt by issuing stock.							
5. Paid accounts payable.							
6. Purchased inventory with cash.							
7. Purchased a one-year insurance policy with cash.							
8. Purchased a long-term investment with cash.							
9. Sold trading securities at a gain.							
10. Sold a machine at a loss.							
11. Retired fully depreciated equipment.							
12. Paid interest on debt.							
13. Purchased available-for-sale securities (long-term).							
14. Received dividend income.							
15. Received cash on account.							
16. Converted bonds to common stock.							
17. Purchased ninety-day Treasury bill.							

687

1. Statement of cash flows prepared

Flanders Corporation
Statement of Cash Flows
For the Year Ended June 30, 20x2

Cash Flows from Operating Activities				
Cash Receipts from Sales				(a)

Schedule of Noncash Investing and Financing Transactions

Chapter 17, P 8. (Continued)

a.	**Cash Receipts from Sales**	=		+				
		=		+				
		=						
b.		=			−			−
		=			−			−
		=						
c.		=		−			−	
		=		−			−	
		=						
d.		=		−				
		=		−				
		=						

Chapter 17, P 8. (Continued)

e.				
f.				
g.				
h.				
i.				
j.				

2. | **Causes of increase in cash identified**

Flanders Corporation's large increase in cash from 20x1 to 20x2 was caused by

a.	
b.	
c.	
d.	
e.	

3. **Computation and assessment of cash flow yield and free cash flow**

Cash Flow Yield	=								
	=		=	**times**					
Free Cash Flow	=								
	=		−		−	$0	+		
	=								

1. Work sheet prepared

O'Brien Corporation
Work Sheet for Statement of Cash Flows
For the Year Ended December 31, 20x2

Description	Account Balances 12/31/x1	Analysis of Transactions		Account Balances 12/31/x2
		Debit	Credit	
Debits				
Total Debits				
Credits				
Total Credits				

Chapter 17, P 9. (Continued)

Description	Account Balances 12/31/x1	Analysis of Transactions		Account Balances 12/31/x2
		Debit	Credit	
Cash Flows from Operating Activities				
Net Income		(a)		

2. Same as solutions to required 1, 2, and 3 in P 6.

1. Statement of cash flows prepared

Hashimi Print Gallery, Inc.
Statement of Cash Flows
For the Year Ended December 31, 20x2

Schedule of Noncash Investing and Financing Transactions

2. **Cash problem explained**

Chapter 17, FRA 1.

Memorandum

Date:	
To:	
From:	
Re:	

At your request, I have prepared an analysis of Tandy Corporation's Statements of Cash Flows. Tandy's Statements of Cash Flows and the computations on which this analysis is based are presented in attachments.

Attachment

All dollar amounts are in millions.

Cash Flow Yield	=	

1998:	=	———	=	**times**

1999:	=	———	=	**times**

Cash Flows to Sales	=	

1998:	=	———	=	

1999:	=	———	=	

Cash Flows to Assets	=	

1998:	=	(	+	) ÷	=

1999:	=	(	+ $1,993.6	) ÷	=

Free Cash Flow	=	

1998:	=	−	−	+
	=			

1999:	=	−	−	+
	=			

Chapter 17, FRA 2.

	Sony:	Canon:

Cash Flow Yield = _____

	Sony			Canon	
1998:	_____ =	times		_____ =	times
1999:	_____ =	times		_____ =	times

Cash Flows to Sales = _____

1998:	_____ =		_____ =
1999:	_____ =		_____ =

Cash Flows to Assets = _____

1998:	_____ =		_____ =
1999:	_____ =		_____ =

Free Cash Flow =

1998:	−	−	=		−	−	=
1999:	−	−	=		−	−	=

1.

2.

3.	The cash-generating efficiency ratios and free cash flow (in millions) for Toys "R" Us for the last three years are as follows:

Cash Flow Yield	=	

1998:	=	———	=		times

1999:	=	———	=		times

2000:	=	———	=		times

Cash Flows to Sales	=	

1998:	=	———	=	

1999:	=	———	=	

2000:	=	———	=	

Cash Flows to Assets	=								
1998:	=							=	
		(		+		)	÷		
1999:	=							=	
		(		+		)	÷		
2000:	=							=	
		(		+		)	÷		
Free Cash Flow	=								
1998:	=		−		−				
	=								
1999:	=		−		−				
	=								
2000:	=		−		−				
	=								

Chapter 18, SE 1.

1.
2.
3.
4.
5.

Chapter 18, SE 2.

1.
2.
3.
4.
5.

Chapter 18, SE 3.

	20x2	20x1	20x0
Net sales			
Accounts receivable (net)			

SiteWorks, Inc. Comparative Income Statements For the Years Ended December 31, 20x1 and 20x0				
			Increase or Decrease	
	20x1	**20x0**	**Amount**	**Percentage**
Net Sales				
Cost of Goods Sold				
Gross Margin				
Operating Expenses				
Operating Income				
Interest Expense				
Income Before Income Taxes				
Income Taxes				
Net Income				
Earnings per share				

SiteWorks, Inc.
Common-Size Balance Sheets
December 31, 20x1 and 20x0

	20x1	20x0
Assets		
Liabilities and Stockholders' Equity		

	20x1	20x0
Current ratio:	= _____ times	= _____ times
Quick ratio:	_____ + _____ + _____ = _____ times	_____ + _____ + _____ = _____ times
	_____	_____
	= _____ − _____ = _____ times	= _____ − _____ = _____ times
	* _____ − _____	** _____ − _____
Receivable turnover:	(_____ + _____) ÷ _____	(_____ + _____) ÷ _____
	= _____ = _____ times	= _____ = _____ times
Average days' sales uncollected:	days _____ = _____ days	days _____ = _____ days
	times	times

(continued)

	20x1	20x0

Inventory turnover:

$$\frac{}{} = \left(+ \right) \div = \text{ times} \qquad = \left(+ \right) \div = \text{ times}$$

Average days' inventory on hand:

$$\frac{}{} = \frac{\text{days}}{\text{times}} = \text{ days} \qquad = \frac{\text{days}}{\text{times}} = \text{ days}$$

Payables turnover:

$$\frac{}{} = \left(+ \right) \div = \text{ times} \qquad = \left(+ \right) \div = \text{ times}$$

Average days' payable:

$$\frac{}{} = \frac{\text{days}}{\text{times}} = \text{ days} \qquad = \frac{\text{days}}{\text{times}} = \text{ days}$$

Profit margin:

20x1					20x0				
	=					=			

Asset turnover:

| (|) ÷ | | = | + | (|) ÷ | | = | + |
| = | times | | | | = | times | | | |

Return on assets:

| = | | | | | = | | | | |

Return on equity:

| (|) ÷ | | = | + | (|) ÷ | | = | + |
| = | | | | | = | | | | |

Debt to equity ratio:

	20x1			20x0		
		+	=		+	=

Interest coverage ratio:

	20x1			20x0		
		=	times		=	times
		+			+	
		=	times		=	times

	20x1	20x0

Cash flow yield:

$$\rule{2cm}{0.4pt} = \rule{2cm}{0.4pt} \text{ times} \qquad \rule{2cm}{0.4pt} = \rule{2cm}{0.4pt} \text{ times}$$

Cash flows to sales:

$$\rule{2cm}{0.4pt} = \rule{2cm}{0.4pt} \qquad \rule{2cm}{0.4pt} = \rule{2cm}{0.4pt}$$

Cash flows to assets:

$$\rule{2cm}{0.4pt} = (\rule{2cm}{0.4pt} + \rule{2cm}{0.4pt}) \div \rule{2cm}{0.4pt} \qquad \rule{2cm}{0.4pt} = (\rule{2cm}{0.4pt} + \rule{2cm}{0.4pt}) \div \rule{2cm}{0.4pt}$$

$$\rule{1cm}{0.4pt} = \rule{1cm}{0.4pt} + \rule{1cm}{0.4pt} = \rule{1cm}{0.4pt} \qquad \rule{1cm}{0.4pt} = \rule{1cm}{0.4pt} + \rule{1cm}{0.4pt} = \rule{1cm}{0.4pt}$$

Free cash flow:

$$\rule{1cm}{0.4pt} = \rule{1cm}{0.4pt} - \rule{1cm}{0.4pt} - \rule{1cm}{0.4pt} \qquad \rule{1cm}{0.4pt} = \rule{1cm}{0.4pt} - \rule{1cm}{0.4pt} - \rule{1cm}{0.4pt}$$

	20x1	20x0
Price/earnings ratio:		
Dividends yield:	= times	= times
	=	=
	* ÷ shares = per share	
*Dividends per share =		

Chapter 18, E 1.

1.		5.		
2.		6.		
3.		7.		
4.				

Chapter 18, E 2.

Fodor Company
Comparative Balance Sheets
December 31, 20x2 and 20x1

	20x2	20x1	Increase or Decrease	
			Amount	Percentage
Assets				
Liabilities and Stockholders' Equity				

Comment:

Chapter 18, E 3.

	20x5	20x4	20x3	20x2	20x1
Net sales					
Cost of goods sold					
General and administrative expenses					
Operating income					

Comment:

Chapter 18, E 4.

Fodor Company
Common-Size Income Statements
For the Years Ended December 31, 20x2 and 20x1

	20x2	20x1
Net Sales		
Cost of Goods Sold		
Gross Margin		
Selling Expenses		
General Expenses		
Total Operating Expenses		
Net Operating Income		

Comment:

Chapter 18, E 5.

	20x2				20x1			
Current ratio	=	times			=	times		
Quick ratio	+	=	+		+	=	+	
	=	times			=	times		
Receivable turnover	(	days ÷	+	) ÷	(	days ÷	+	) ÷
		times				times		
	=	times			=	times		
Average days' sales uncollected	=	days			=	days		
Inventory turnover	(	days ÷	+	) ÷	(	days ÷	+	) ÷
		times				times		
	=	times			=	times		
Average days' inventory on hand	=	days			=	days		
Payables turnover	(	days +	+	) ÷	(	days −	+	) ÷
		times				times		
	=	times			=	times		
Average days' payable	=	days			=	days		

Comment:

713

Receivable Turnover

Year	Net Sales					Average Accounts Receivable	
20x1:	(	+	)	÷	=		times
20x2:	(	+	)	÷	=		times
20x3:	(	+	)	÷	=		times
20x4:	(	+	)	÷	=		times

Payables Turnover

	Cost of Goods Sold +/– Change in Inventories					Average Accounts Payable	
20x1:	(– +	)	÷	=			times
20x2:	(+ +	)	÷	=			times
20x3:	(+ +	)	÷	=			times
20x4:	(+ +	)	÷	=			times

Inventory Turnover

	Cost of Goods Sold					Average Inventory	
20x1:	(	+	)	÷	=		times
20x2:	(	+	)	÷	=		times
20x3:	(	+	)	÷	=		times
20x4:	(	+	)	÷	=		times

	20x2				20x1		
Profit margin	(=				=)		
	=				=		
Asset turnover	(=	+	) ÷		(=	+	) ÷
	=	=	times		=	=	times
Return on assets	(=	+	) ÷		(=	+	) ÷
	=	=			=	=	
Return on equity*	(=	+	) ÷		(=	+	) ÷
	=	=			=	=	

* In each year, equity equals 60 percent (1.00 ÷ 1.67) of total assets because the debt to equity ratio is .67.

	Company F				Company G			
Debt to equity ratio		*	=	times		*	=	times
	*		—		*		—	
Interest coverage ratio		+				+		
	=	times			=	times		
P/E ratio	=		=	times	=		=	times
Dividends yield		=				=		

Comment:

716

Cash flow yield		————	=	**times**
Cash flows to sales	=	————	=	
Cash flows to assets		(	+	) ÷
	=	————	=	
Free cash flow		−	−	
	=			

1. **Schedules showing amount and percentage changes prepared**

			Increase or Decrease	
Sanborn Corporation **Comparative Income Statements** **For the Years Ended December 31, 20x2 and 20x1** **(in thousands of dollars)**				
	20x2	**20x1**	**Amount**	**Percentage**

			Increase or Decrease	
Sanborn Corporation **Comparative Balance Sheets** **December 31, 20x2 and 20x1** **(in thousands of dollars)**				
	20x2	**20x1**	**Amount**	**Percentage**
Assets				
Liabilities and **Stockholders' Equity**				

2. | **Common-size income statements and balance sheet prepared**

Sanborn Corporation
Common-Size Income Statements
For the Years Ended December 31, 20x2 and 20x1

	20x2	20x1

Sanborn Corporation
Common-Size Balance Sheets
December 31, 20x2 and 20x1

	20x2	20x1
Assets		
Liabilities and Stockholders' Equity		

3. **Results commented on**

Transaction	Ratio	Effect		
		Increase	Decrease	None
a. Sold merchandise on account.	Current ratio			
b. Sold merchandise on account.	Inventory turnover			
c. Collected on accounts receivable.	Quick ratio			
d. Wrote off an uncollectible account.	Receivable turnover			
e. Paid on accounts payable.	Current ratio			
f. Declared cash dividend.	Return on equity			
g. Incurred advertising expense.	Profit margin			
h. Issued stock dividend.	Debt to equity ratio			
i. Issued bond payable.	Asset turnover			
j. Accrued interest expense.	Current ratio			
k. Paid previously declared cash dividend.	Dividends yield			
l. Purchased treasury stock.	Return on assets			
m. Recorded depreciation expense.	Cash flow yield			

Ratio	20x2	20x1	Favorable (F) or Unfavorable (U) Change
1. Liquidity analysis			
a. Current ratio	_____ = _____ + _____ + _____ = _____ times	_____ + _____ + _____ = _____ times	
b. Quick ratio	_____ = _____ + _____ + _____ = _____ times	_____ + _____ + _____ = _____ = _____ times	
c. Receivable turnover	(_____ + _____) ÷ _____ = _____ times	(_____ + _____) ÷ _____ = _____ times	
d. Average days' sales uncollected	_____ days = _____ days ÷ _____ times	_____ days = _____ days ÷ _____ times	
e. Inventory turnover	(_____ + _____) ÷ _____ = _____ times	(_____ + _____) ÷ _____ = _____ times	
f. Average days' inventory on hand	_____ days = _____ days ÷ _____ times	_____ days = _____ days ÷ _____ times	
g. Payables turnover	(_____ − _____ + _____) ÷ _____ = _____ times	(_____ + _____) ÷ _____ = _____ times	
h. Average days' payable	_____ days = _____ days ÷ _____ times	_____ days = _____ days ÷ _____ times	

Note: All amounts used in calculating the ratios and percentages are in thousands of dollars except the amounts used to calculate the P/E ratio and the denominator in the dividends yield.

723

Ratio	20x2	20x1	Favorable (F) or Unfavorable (U) Change
2. Profitability analysis			
a. Profit margin	=	=	
b. Asset turnover	(____ + ____) ÷ ____ = ____ times	(____ + ____) ÷ ____ = ____ times	
c. Return on assets	(____ + ____) ÷ ____ =	(____ + ____) ÷ ____ =	
d. Return on equity	(____ + ____) ÷ ____ =	(____ + ____) ÷ ____ =	
3. Long-term solvency analysis			
a. Debt to equity ratio	____ + ____ + ____ =	____ + ____ + ____ =	
b. Interest coverage ratio	____ = ____ times	____ = ____ times	

Ratio	20x2	20x1	Favorable (F) or Unfavorable (U) Change
4. Cash flow adequacy analysis			
a. Cash flow yield	$\dfrac{\quad}{\quad}$ = times	$\dfrac{\quad}{\quad}$ = times	
b. Cash flows to sales	$\dfrac{\quad}{\quad}$ =	$\dfrac{\quad}{\quad}$ =	
c. Cash flows to assets	$\dfrac{\quad}{(\quad + \quad) \div \quad}$ =	$\dfrac{\quad}{(\quad + \quad) \div \quad}$ =	
d. Free cash flow	$\quad - \quad - \quad - \quad =$	$\quad - \quad - \quad - \quad =$	
5. Market strength analysis			
a. Price/earnings ratio	$\dfrac{\quad}{\quad}$ = times	$\dfrac{\quad}{\quad}$ = times	
b. Dividends yield	$\dfrac{\quad \div \quad \text{shares}}{\quad}$ =	$\dfrac{\quad \div \quad \text{shares}}{\quad}$ =	

Ratio	Lewis Corporation	Ramsey Corporation	6. Company with More Favorable Ratio
1. Liquidity analysis			
a. Current ratio	___ + ___ + ___ = ___ + ___ + ___ times	___ + ___ + ___ = ___ + ___ + ___ times	
b. Quick ratio	___ = ___ + ___ = ___ times	___ = ___ + ___ = ___ times	
c. Receivable turnover	___ = ___ times	___ = ___ times	
d. Average days' sales uncollected	times ___ = ___ days	times ___ = ___ days	
e. Inventory turnover	___ = ___ times	___ = ___ times	
f. Average days' inventory on hand	days ___ times ___ = ___ days	days ___ times ___ = ___ days	
g. Payables turnover	___ + $0 ___ = ___ times	___ + $0 ___ = ___ times	
h. Average days' payable	days ___ times ___ = ___ days	days ___ times ___ = ___ days	

(continued)

Ratio	Lewis Corporation	Ramsey Corporation	6. Company with More Favorable Ratio
2. Profitability analysis			
a. Profit margin	____ = ____	____ = ____	
b. Asset turnover	____ = ____ times	____ = ____ times	
c. Return on assets	____ = ____	____ = ____	
d. Return on equity	____ ÷ ____ = ____ = ____	____ ÷ ____ = ____ = ____	
3. Long-term solvency analysis			
a. Debt to equity ratio	____ ÷ ____ + ____ + ____ = ____ times	____ ÷ ____ + ____ + ____ = ____ times	
b. Interest coverage ratio	____ + ____ = ____ times	____ + ____ = ____ times	

(continued)

Ratio	Lewis Corporation	Ramsey Corporation	6. Company with More Favorable Ratio
4. Cash flow adequacy analysis			
a. Cash flow yield	= ___ times	= ___ times	
b. Cash flows to sales	___ = ___ =	___ = ___ =	
c. Cash flows to assets	___ = ___ =	___ = ___ =	
d. Free cash flow	___ - ___ - ___ - ___ =	___ - ___ - ___ - ___ =	
5. Market strength analysis			
a. Price/earnings ratio	___ = ___ = ___ times	___ = ___ = ___ times	
b. Dividends yield	___ ÷ ___ shares =	___ ÷ ___ shares =	

7. Use of information from prior years

728

Transaction	Ratio	Effect		
		Increase	Decrease	None
a. Issued common stock for cash.	Asset turnover			
b. Declared cash dividend.	Current ratio			
c. Sold treasury stock.	Return on equity			
d. Borrowed cash by issuing note payable.	Debt to equity ratio			
e. Paid salaries expense.	Inventory turnover			
f. Purchased merchandise for cash.	Current ratio			
g. Sold equipment for cash.	Receivable turnover			
h. Sold merchandise on account.	Quick ratio			
i. Paid current portion of long-term debt.	Return on assets			
j. Gave sales discount.	Profit margin			
k. Purchased marketable securities for cash.	Quick ratio			
l. Declared 5 percent stock dividend.	Current ratio			
m. Purchased a building.	Free cash flow			

Ratio	20x2	20x1	Favorable (F) or Unfavorable (U) Change
1. Liquidity analysis			
a. Current ratio	___ + ___ + ___ = ___ times	___ + ___ + ___ = ___ times	
b. Quick ratio	(___ + ___ + ___) ÷ ___ = ___ times	(___ + ___ + ___) ÷ ___ = ___ times	
c. Receivable turnover	(___ + ___) ÷ ___ = ___ times	(___ + ___) ÷ ___ = ___ times	
d. Average days' sales uncollected	___ days = ___ times	___ days = ___ times	
e. Inventory turnover	(___ + ___) ÷ ___ = ___ times	(___ + ___) ÷ ___ = ___ times	
f. Average days' inventory on hand	___ days = ___ times	___ days = ___ times	
g. Payables turnover	(___ + ___) ÷ ___ = ___ times	(___ + ___) ÷ ___ = ___ times	
h. Average days' payable	___ days = ___ days	___ days = ___ days	

Note: All amounts used in calculating the ratios and percentages are in thousands of dollars, except the amounts used to calculate the P/E ratio and the dividends yield.

Ratio	20x2	20x1	Favorable (F) or Unfavorable (U) Change*
2. Profitability analysis			
a. Profit margin	___ = ___ =	___ = ___ =	
b. Asset turnover	___ = (___ + ___) ÷ ___ = ___ times	___ = (___ + ___) ÷ ___ = ___ times	
c. Return on assets	___ = (___ + ___) ÷ ___ =	___ = (___ + ___) ÷ ___ =	
d. Return on equity	___ = (___ + ___) ÷ ___ =	___ = (___ + ___) ÷ ___ =	
3. Long-term solvency analysis			
a. Debt to equity ratio	___ + ___ = ___ + ___ = ___ times	___ + ___ = ___ + ___ = ___ times	
b. Interest coverage ratio	___ + ___ = ___ + ___ = ___ times	___ + ___ = ___ + ___ = ___ times	

(continued)

731

Ratio	20x2	20x1	Favorable (F) or Unfavorable (U) Change*
4. Cash flow adequacy analysis			
a. Cash flow yield	= times	= times	
b. Cash flows to sales	=	=	
c. Cash flows to assets	(+) ÷ =	(+) ÷ =	
d. Free cash flow	= − −	= − −	
5. Market strength analysis			
a. Price/earnings ratio	= times	= times	
b. Dividends yield	÷ shares =	÷ shares =	

Chapter 18, SD 2.

Based on Exhibit 1, Goodyear's business segments are tires, engineered products, and chemical products. The relative size of the segments in terms of sales and income for 1999 are as follows (amounts in millions):

Segment	Sales		Income	
	Amount	Percentage	Amount	Percentage
Totals				

This measure for the three segments is as follows:

Tires		(		÷		)
		(		÷		)
		(		÷		)

Most (56.7%) of Goodyear's tire sales are in North America. The most profitable region in terms of return on assets, however, is Latin American Tire, as shown by the following computations:

North American Tire		(		÷		)
Europe Tire		(		÷		)
Eastern Europe, Africa, and Middle East Tire		(		÷		)
Latin American Tire		(		÷		)
Asia Tire		(		÷		)

Chapter 18, SD 6.		
1. **Common-size income statements, profit margin, and return on equity**		
		Unforgettable
	Apple a Day	**Edibles**
Net Sales		

2. **Results discussed**	

Chapter 18, FRA 1.

Summary of Operations	1999	1998	1997	1996	1995
Sales					
Cost of products sold					
Interest expense					
Provision for income taxes					
Net income					
Dividends Paid: Common					
Total assets					
Total debt					
Shareholders' equity					

Chapter 18, FRA 2.

	Pfizer	Roche
Receivable turnover	= (___ + ___) ÷ ___ = ___ times	= (___ + ___) ÷ ___ = ___ times
Average days' sales uncollected	= ___ days / ___ times = ___ days	= ___ days / ___ times = ___ days
Inventory turnover	= ___ ÷ (___ + ___) = ___ times	= ___ ÷ (___ + ___) = ___ times
Average days' inventory on hand	= ___ days / ___ times = ___ days	= ___ days / ___ times = ___ days
Payables turnover	= ___ ÷ (___ + ___ − ___) = ___ times	= ___ ÷ (___ + ___ + ___) = ___ times
Average days' payable	= ___ days / ___ times = ___ days	= ___ days / ___ times = ___ days
Operating cycle	= ___ + ___ = ___ days	= ___ + ___ = ___ days
Days of financing required	= ___ − ___ = ___ days	= ___ − ___ = ___ days

736

Chapter 18, FRA 3.

All computations are for the years ended January 29, 2000, and January 30, 1999 (in millions).

Liquidity ratios and analysis of Toys "R" Us

	2000			1999		
Current ratio	_____	=	times	_____	=	times
Quick ratio	____ + ____			____ + ____		
	= _____	=	times	= _____	=	times
Receivable turnover	= _____			= _____		
	(____ + ____) ÷			(____ + ____) ÷		
	= _____	=	times	= _____	=	times
Average days' sales uncollected	days / times	=	days	days / times	=	days
Inventory turnover	= _____			= _____		
	(____ + ____) ÷			(____ + ____) ÷		
	= _____	=	times	= _____	=	times
Average days' inventory on hand	days / times	=	days	days / times	=	days
Payables turnover	____ + ____			____ − ____		
	(____ + ____) ÷			(____ + ____) ÷		
	= _____	=	times	= _____	=	times
Average days' payable	days / times	=	days	days / times	=	days

Profitability ratios and analysis of Toys "R" Us

	2000	1999
Profit margin	——— =	——— =
Asset turnover	= ——— (+) ÷	= ——— (+) ÷
	= ——— = times	= ——— = times
Return on assets	——— =	——— =
Return on equity	= ——— (+) ÷	= ——— (+) ÷
	= ——— =	= ——— =

Long-term solvency ratios and analysis of Toys "R" Us

	2000				1999			
Debt to equity ratio	_____	=		times		_____	=		times
Interest coverage ratio	_____	+		=	times	_____	+		=	times

Cash flow adequacy ratios and analysis of Toys "R" Us

	2000				1999			
Cash flow yield	_____	=		times		_____	=		times
Cash flows to sales	_____	=				_____	=		
Cash flows to assets	=	_____				=	_____		
		(	+	) ÷			(	+	) ÷
	=	_____	=			=	_____	=	
Free cash flow		−	$0	−			−	$0	−
	=					=			

Chapter 18, FRA 3. (Continued)

Market strength ratios and analysis of Toys "R" Us

	2000				1999			
Price/earnings ratio		* =		times		* =		times
Dividends yield								
* **2000:** (		+		)	÷			
1999: (		+		)	÷			

Appendix A, P 1.

Part A

	Purchased special-purpose machine for DM 50,000							
	DM		x	$0.55	=			
	Made payment of accounts payable of DM 50,000							
	DM		x		=			

Part B

Nov.	15							
			Made sale to U.K. Company in pounds					
				x	$1.70	=		
Dec.	31							
			Recorded exchange loss due to decrease in value of British pound					
				x		=		
				−		=		
Feb.	15							
			Collected on account and recognized exchange gain due to increase in value of British pound					
				x		=		

May	15				
	17				
			Sale, terms n/30, payment to be DM 300,000		
			÷		
	21				
			Purchase, terms n/30, payment to be 1,200,000 pesos		
			÷		
	25				
	31				
			Sale, terms n/60, payment to be 400,000,000 lire		
			÷		
June	5				
	7				
			Purchase, terms n/30, payment to be ¥26,000,000		
			÷		

June	15					
	16					
				Collection on account in marks		
				DM	x	
	17					
	20					
				Payment on account in pesos		
				pesos x		
				=		
	22					
				Sale, terms n/30, payment to		
				be £60,000		
				÷		
	30					
				Recorded adjustment for incomplete		
				transaction of May 31		
				lire x	=	
				−	=	

June	30										
			Recorded adjustment for incomplete transaction of June 7								
				X			=				
				−			=				
	30										
			Recorded adjustment for incomplete transaction of June 22								
				X		=					
				−			=				
July	7										
			Made payment on account in yen								
				X			=				
	19										
	22										
			Collection on account in dollars								
				X		=					
	30										
			Collection on account in lire								
				lire	X			=			

Appendix B, P 1.   B-1

1.

2.

3.

4.

5.

6.

B-1

20x0					
Apr.	1				
June	1				
Sept.	1				
			Received cash dividend from Season Company		
			shares x =		
Nov.	1				
Dec.	31				
			Recorded reduction of investment portfolio to market		
			— =		

Company	Shares	Market	Total	Cost
Season				
Abbado				
Frankel				
Totals				

Appendix B, P 2. (Continued)

20x1							
Feb.	1						
May	1						
Sept.	1						
			Received cash dividend from Season Company				
			shares	x		=	
Dec.	31						
			Adjusted allowance to increase long-term investments to market because market now exceeds cost				
			−		=		
			Company	Shares	Market	Total	Cost
			Season				
			Abbado				
			Frankel				
			Totals				

1. **Entries in journal form prepared**

Quarter					
1					
1					
			Recorded cash dividend from Vivanco Company		
			40% x ____ = ____		
2					
2					
3					
3					
4					
4					

Appendix B, P 3. (Continued)

2. T account prepared

Investment in Vivanco Company			
Bal.			
Bal.			

Appendix C, E 1.

(1) Simple interest

	X	12%	=	

(2) Compounded semiannually

	X		=	
	X		=	

(3) Compounded quarterly at 3% for 4 periods (see Table 1 in the appendix on future value and present value tables)

	X		=	

(4) Compounded monthly at 1% for 12 periods (see Table 1 in the appendix on future value and present value tables)

	X		=	

Appendix C, E 2.

(1) Single payment of $20,000 at 7% for 10 years (see Table 1 in the appendix on future value and present value tables)

	X		=	

(2) Ten annual payments of $2,000 at 7% (see Table 2 in the appendix on future value and present value tables)

	X		=	

(3) Single payment of $6,000 at 9% for 7 years (see Table 1 in the appendix on future value and present value tables)

	X		=	

(4) Seven annual payments of $6,000 at 9% (see Table 2 in the appendix on future value and present value tables)

	X		=	

Appendix C, E 3.

(1) Compounded annually (see Table 1 in the appendix on future value and present value tables)

	X		=	

(2) Compounded semiannually at 4% for 14 periods (see Table 1 in the appendix on future value and present value tables)

	X		=	

(3) Compounded quarterly at 2% for 28 periods (see Table 1 in the appendix on future value and present value tables)

	X		=	

Appendix C, E 4.

(1) 10% compounded annually (see Table 2 in the appendix on future value and present value tables)

	X		=	

(2) 10% compounded semiannually

Year	Balance		Rate		Interest	Deposits
1		X	0.05	=		
1		X		=		
2		X		=		
2		X		=		
3		X		=		
3		X		=		
4		X		=		
4		X		=		
End of year 4						

You can find the same result more directly by calculating the annual simple interest rate equal to 10 percent compounded semiannually, using Table 2 in the appendix on future value and present value tables to extrapolate a table factor for that simple interest rate, and completing the problem as we did in 1 above.

Appendix C, E 4. (Continued)

	To calculate the simple interest rate, remember that saying that we increase a number by 5 percent is the same as saying that we multiply it by 1.05 (1 + 5%). Over two semiannual periods, we will have multiplied our original amount by 1.05 squared. The simple annual interest rate equivalent to 10 percent compounded semiannually will be (1.05) squared minus one.		

(1.05)^2 − 1 = 10.25%

To extrapolate a table factor for 10.25 percent over four periods, take the table factors for 10 percent and 12 percent and add 12.5 percent of the difference between them [.25 ÷ (12 − 10)] to the factors for 10 percent.

Difference			
	X		
	+		
10.25%			
	X		
			(Note minor difference due to rounding.)

(3) 4% compounded annually (see Table 2 in the appendix on future value and present value tables)

	X		=

Appendix C, E 4. (Continued)

(4) 16% compounded quarterly*

Year	Balance		Rate		Interest	Deposits
1		x	0.04	=		
1		x		=		
1		x		=		
1		x		=		
2		x		=		
2		x		=		
2		x		=		
2		x		=		
3		x		=		
3		x		=		
3		x		=		
3		x		=		
4		x		=		
4		x		=		
4		x		=		
4		x		=		
End of year 4						

* **This part may also be computed in the same way as is done in (2).**

Appendix C, E 5.

a. Required rate of return, $20,000 invested, $40,000 needed in 12 years

To find table factor, for use with Table 1 in the appendix on future value and present value tables:

	÷		=	

To find interest rate for which table factor after 12 years equals 2.000:

Rate	Factor
Difference	
?%	
Difference	
÷	

Required rate of return is	

b. Time required for $40,000 at 7% to accumulate to $64,000

To find table factor, for use with Table 1 in the appendix on future value and present value tables:

	÷		=	

To find number of periods for which table factor at 7% equals 1.600:

Periods	Factor
	.
Difference	
?	
Difference	
÷	

Pruitt must wait		years to buy his summer home.

Appendix C, E 6.

Table factor for the amount of $1 paid in each period, for 4 years at 8%:

		÷		=	

Appendix C, E 7.

			annual rent
	x		factor, from Table 4 in the appendix on future value and present value tables, for present value of $1 per period, for 5 periods at 8%
			present value of rent to be paid for 5 years

Saber should expect to pay | | . |

Appendix C, E 8.

(1) Single payment of $24,000 at 6% for 12 years (see Table 3 in the appendix on future value and present value tables)

	x	0.497	=	

(2) Annual payments of $2,000 at 6% for 12 years (see Table 4 in the appendix on future value and present value tables)

	x		=	

(3) Single payment of $5,000 at 9% for 5 years (see Table 3 in the appendix on future value and present value tables)

	x		=	

(4) Five annual payments of $5,000 at 9% (see Table 4 in the appendix on future value and present value tables)

	x		=	

Appendix C, E 9.

	Years	Rate	Factor from Table 3*			Present Value of $60,000	
(1)				x	$60,000	=	
(2)				x		=	
(3)				x		=	
(4)				x		=	

Appendix C, E 10.

	Pay-ments	Rate	Factor from Table 4*			Present Value of $1,200 Payments	
(1)				x		=	
(2)				x		=	
(3)				x		=	
(4)				x		=	

*In the appendix on future value and present value tables.

Appendix C, E 11.

To calculate the present value of the note:

Factor for present value of $1 at 12% for 2 years, from Table 3 in the appendix on future value and present value tables:

		x	
Present value		=	

To calculate discount on note:

		−
Discount	=	

To calculate annual interest:

Year	Beginning Balance	Annual Interest		Ending Balance
1			*	
2			**	

*		X		=	
**		X		=	

Adjusted interest expense for year 2 will be:

1. | **To record purchase on Pendleton records and sale on Leyland records**

Pendleton Journal

Leyland Journal

2. | **To adjust interest expense and interest income at the end of first year**

Pendleton Journal

Leyland Journal

3. | **To record interest expense and interest income and payment of the note at the end of the second year**

Pendleton Journal

Leyland Journal

Appendix C, E 12.

To find the present value of the purchase transaction:

			annual net cash flow
	x		factor, from Table 4 in the appendix on future value and present value tables, for 8 years at 14%
			present value of net cash flows
–			less machine purchase price
			present value of transaction

Appendix C, E 13.

Since the 16 percent annual interest is compounded quarterly, the applicable interest rate is 4 percent (16 percent ÷ 4 quarters in a year) and the number of periods is 3 (9 months ÷ 3 months in a quarter). The purchase (sale) price is computed as follows (see Table 3 in the appendix on future value and present value tables):

	Future payment		Factor (3 periods, 4%)		Present Value	
		x		=		
		x		=		

The entries necessary to record the purchase and subsequent payment in Borst's records are as follows:

Jan.	1				
			Purchased tool machine		
Oct.	1				
			Paid on account plus imputed interest expense		

Appendix C, E 13. (Continued)

The entries necessary to record the sale and subsequent receipt in Johnson's records are as follows:

Jan.	1				
Oct.	1				

Appendix C, E 14.

From Table 1 in the appendix on future value and present value tables, the future value factor is based on nine monthly periods at 1 percent (12 percent divided by 12 months).

Investment	x	Factor (9 periods, 1%)	=	Future Value	
	x		=		
Jan.	1				
Feb.	1				
		Earned one month's interest income			
		x	0.01	=	
Mar.	1				
		Earned one month's interest income			
		x		=	

Appendix C, E 15.

See Table 2 in the appendix on future value and present value tables.

Future value of fund	÷	Factor (4 periods, 10%)	=	Annual Investment
	÷		=	(rounded)

Journal entry:

Appendix C, E 16.

Raftson's offer to sell:

From Table 4 in the appendix on future value and present value tables:

Periodic Cash Flow	x	Factor (20 periods, 12%)	=	Present Value
	x		=	

Ruiz's offer to buy:

From Table 4 in the appendix on future value and present value tables:

Periodic Cash Flow	x	Factor (10 periods, 12%)	=	Present Value
	x		=	

The range between the offer to sell and the offer to buy is from $_____ to $_____ .